Growth Through Grief

A Powerful Story Through Loss and Stepping Forward

By
Ric Hart

Grosvenor House
Publishing Limited

This book is published by
Grosvenor House Publishing Ltd
Link House
140 The Broadway, Tolworth, Surrey, KT6 7HT.
www.grosvenorhousepublishing.co.uk

A CIP record for this book
is available from the British Library

Paperback ISBN 978-1-80381-490-2
Hardback ISBN 978-1-80381-491-9
eBook ISBN 978-1-80381-492-6

Introduction

They do say grief is seven stages: shock, denial, anger, bargaining, depression, acceptance/hope, and processing grief. For me personally, this was not a set process from one to the next. I felt like it was a circle, constantly going around... back and forth, or like levels. You would level up, then get pushed right back to the beginning or back to a certain element, from depression back to anger... anger to denial.

From Jade's death, through to the circumstances around her care and learning about something new as time went on, new emails, new information, new visuals. This didn't help as it added to what I experienced, which was the grieving process, going back and forth or round and round, alongside trauma.

However, I do believe when you step into acceptance, you are past most of the others. I've learned, though, that you can be in acceptance for as long as possible. It doesn't matter how long, but if you ever get to this point, then I believe it's a miracle or even healing. My journey through this book shares my emotions and state of mind month on month for 50 months, hopefully giving you, the reader, a flavour of this. It shares most of my thoughts and feelings, and what was happening as a domino effect throughout my deep grief and ongoing grief.

I never knew the power of breaking things and time down until post-July 2018. The moments following the loss of my wife, Jade, mother of my son. The power of taking small steps, the power of taking what looks like a mountain to climb, into just taking the first step, then the second. Being engrossed in each step, and trust me, there is enormous energy, strength, and power in this process.

Before July 2018, my life was complete with love, happiness, and fulfilment. I lived a very fast, happy, busy life with Jade. We lived for today but tried to have one eye on the future, travelling the world yearly as much as we could; we had a very successful life together. Our happiest moment was in October 2017, when we found out Jade was pregnant, and in July 2018, in the first moments of the birth of Hugo Hart. This was a moment that changed my life forever, but certainly not forgetting our movie star wedding in Thailand. In the blink of an eye, just like that, Jade was taken from us through horrific tragedy. She lost her son, her husband, her family and friends, her career, her social life, everything. Everyone lost someone extremely special, and I'm sure she has left a huge hole in people's lives, and this continues both now and forever.

But it's how we view our loss, what we do to make our lost loved ones proud and make ourselves proud. This allows us to view grief with as much good feeling as possible. I wasn't just going to move through my grief and step forward, I was going to do something completely different that would allow Jade to live on in a very special way.

I had lost my soulmate, my wife, my lover, my best friend, in our everyday lives, and Hugo lost his mummy. Having a mother full stop, the love of a mother, that female touch, that female connection. The emotions, love and comfort a mother brings within a family are massive. As a single father stepping forward from day one with my son, I knew how much I had to do. It felt like an impossible mountain to climb, but I needed to focus on looking up, the psychological importance of this, putting one foot in front of the other as much as I could.

I 100% fell deep into survival mode in my early days of losing Jade. My loss should not have happened. Why us? Why Jade? Looking back now, I was suffering from shock and trauma. I didn't believe what was happening; the focus was on my son needs to sleep well and to be fed every two hours, with tens of nappy changes daily. My adrenaline and inner strength were being put to a major test, one that no one should have to face alone or even have to go through. When I was in ICU, I looked out the window and said deep within my soul, "You have to make Jade proud, Ric, you have to; she deserves this 100%. Be the best father and mother you can be in Jade's absence because that is your job."

'Be the best you can be' stamped on my forehead resonates from that moment in time. I placed Hugo beside Jade on the bed in ICU and looked upon them both in floods of tears. I took a photo which held huge significance then, but it also became a symbol of how I measured my strength and where my emotions were going forward – something I will share at the end of the book with you. I remember looking back now, thinking about the past, the future and going back and forth like a yo-yo; it was so overwhelming and created anxiety at its highest. It moved me into deep depression very quickly. I knew I had to find a way to be in the present, I knew I needed to stop looking for that mountain tip through the clouds, and I needed to keep my feet on the ground and take each hour as it came.

Breaking time down for me worked. I always asked myself, what am I doing to put me in a better place within the next hour or so. Of course, it didn't always go like this, as my rollercoaster of grief involved so many rocky roads. Trust me, it's unreal. Again, no one should have to face what has been thrown at me in the last four to five years.

This book is no answer to grief and the process, but it is a snapshot of my grief and story. It covers my growth and decisions made, which I hope helps you, the reader, on your journey or just inspires you to make better decisions to find growth through grief or even growth through adversity.

How do you gain more energy from having two to three hours' sleep a night, week after week, month after month? Feeding your son every two hours, alongside him, cleaning him, changing him, just watching him all the time, making sure he's breathing? Dealing with deep grief, trauma, loss, tragedy, sadness, and just getting through each day. Some might say *get help and sleep more*. I had lots of support, family and friends coming round at the start to help where they could, which I appreciated more than ever. But I knew I had to take this journey alone as much as I could, as I knew this would grow me, my life and my belief in myself.

Some may say more sleep would help, but I decided to take a different path, I decided to run, run far, run away from my life, and that's what I did. When Hugo was with family for a few hours, and when he was in nursery after five or six months, I decided to (in that small window) run for hours, processing everything, where my body was at 160 beats per minute, in the countryside, looking out to the world, always working it all out in my mind. Having a vision for my steps through my grief, which turned out to be very powerful ones.

My running helped me through my deep grief. It allowed me to release all my anxiety, emotions, and thoughts to the world, to then manifest what I wanted to do and how I wanted to do it. I had a vision, and when Ric Hart has a vision where all my body tingles, wow, I go at things with all my heart. I was never going to fail. In short, I ran many 10Ks, a half marathon and a full marathon in memory of Jade. Never did I think I would be running this marathon in memory of her. As I had said when she was alive, *I will do this for you, as you did nine months growing our son*, I will train for nine months and run a marathon. This helped me within the first 18 months of my loss, giving me great focus, bringing people together, and doing something very special for someone who will remain in our hearts forever. I ran the marathon solo, and this represented the knowledge that I needed to take my own journey. A journey of tragedy, a journey of being reborn, a journey of growth, my own steps towards finding acceptance and peace in my life through the most horrific reality. *Could I do this?* I asked myself. *Now it's time to really believe in who you are...* I had to believe I was superhuman, with a greater force out there pushing me on through my next steps.

The pandemic hit in March 2020, and this took me back into deep grief. 22 to 23 months in from my loss: no social contact, not much communication with the outside world, and having to deal with a nearly two-year-old boy, which, trust me, was probably the most challenging times of parenthood. I do believe there is a blessing in everything, and I'm a very positive glass-half-full type of guy, so I always focused on what and where the blessing was. Looking back now, the pandemic was a process through my grief, a process through my ideas. That was my time to act on all the ideas in my head, which was my blessing. What looked like one of my hardest challenges gave me the opportunity to grow through it and keep on growing. I will say this, though, it is unlikely you will ever again come across a man who lost his wife hours after birth, with part of that horrific process going through a pandemic. The steps I took and my journey holds a huge level of rarity. So, what did I do...? I turned to writing and bringing all my journaling together, and turned to poetry and image ideas that were in my head from running. Now to some people, my ideas would have been crazy, but to me, it was my journey. To leave a legacy, to grow through grief, to do something special for Hugo, and maybe help someone else out there.

If someone said to me five years ago, *Ric, you are going to write five children's books and two adult books and will have got them all published in the space of three years*, I would be saying, "Get out of town... lol."

That is because I am the guy who last year was tested for dyslexia and was diagnosed with quite a form of it. I am the guy who struggles to enjoy reading books – by page two, I'm gone! I can read, but not fast, and my English literature is poor. I am no poet and am not very good at using words for description, and also find it difficult to understand what some large words mean, and sometimes even basic. When writing also, it all can look like mish mash and sometimes I write letters down that are further on in the word, so I have to start again, because my mind is like over drive, thank god for computers lol. So, when I look back now at the steps I took, the challenge I set myself, I have to say, "Wow!" If I can do it, so can you!

In short, I fast-forward now to November 2022: two and a half years later from my ideas stage, but pretty much two years on from my first publishing date, marking five children's bereavement books published, my autobiography about mine and Jade's life, ending with my loss and steps through grief going forward.

I'm a non-profit book author, and all my books have been placed with local and national charities to help similar causes and to give back. What this did for me inside was phenomenal. I can't express the warm, happy

ιis gave me, becoming a book author and doing
ιg special from every angle. This was for sure
αιισιιισ huge piece to my jigsaw and steps growing
through grief. From all the sketches to the ideas, the
poetry, the changes along the way, the new ideas from
book one to book five in the children's book world
and writing *Pupy Love*, I look back now and just say,
"Wow!"

With all the inspiration I gained along the way, taking
action was a no-brainer, and that key word ACTION,
there's some power in this, people. If we don't take
that step through change and do our best to adapt
and think outside the box, the world is going to
swallow us up and spit us out. That was not going to
happen with me, not a chance. Looking back now:
creating my books; Jade's website; Jade's Facebook
page for *Pupy Love*; creating Hugo and Jade's
Christmas card; attaching all my books to charities;
creating Hugo's superhero website for his superhero
book and merchandise page; trademarking a very
special symbol; even getting it tattooed on my arm,
and it looks great – I couldn't be prouder. I did it in
style. I was taking different steps than most through
grief, for example: publishing seven books within three
years, creating everlasting websites, and all that I have
created for Hugo to carry forward into his family. My
focus has just been remarkable throughout my journey,
to find a way to self-heal, to find my way to acceptance,
which is where lots who have lost find it very hard to
get to. I will share my final thoughts around this at the
end of this book.

I have also created our very own YouTube channel, sharing our holidays and travels abroad to date, going away together as Hugo and Daddy.

'Hugo and Daddy's Real-Life Adventures' another great idea for both of us, but also for Hugo to find inspiration one day from all I have created. I also talk openly about what's important to me and my feelings and life on my Instagram 'Real with Ric' alongside mine and my son's journey but also injecting motivation and inspiration into others. This helps me so much: to talk, share and be an example that it's OK for men especially to talk out, share and be honest. Growth through grief can be defined as a hundred and one things, as little as: I don't feel guilty anymore for being me, or finding me again; smiling and having a good time – to so many different things – it's crazy. My journey was very different, as is all of our journeys, but my steps taken were to grow beyond and out of a very dark place.

I was inspired to write this book through sharing a bird's eye view and my emotions, month on month and growth through my journey in a snap. I know this has helped me, placing me in a stronger place and hopefully helping someone else out there. It's a representation of sharing, talking out, what was happening through my process of grief, which again isn't the answer to growing through grief, but my own personal story. I hope you resonate with the book, the quotes, and the feel the book gives, but if not, that's still OK. I want to leave you with the knowledge there is always HOPE – we just have to believe deep down. How we feel, how we visualise, and gaining that electrifying feeling inside, we only have to take the first step, and be engrossed in our journey allowing our why and purpose to shine on even more as time passes. An amazing illustration at the back of the book shows this through my journey and what was important to me wrapping around my grief, creating good feeling and growth along the way.

Contents

July 2018 – The moment of death

"When you are faced with your darkest day on this planet, keeping your head up literally and just focusing on one foot in front of the other: this is key. Keep moving."

After the birth of our son, our first and only, Hugo Jaden Hart, on 8 July 2018, we both could not have been happier. What a moment in life that most can relate to. Life felt perfect; this was the missing link and certainly the best chapter to date. The missing piece to the jigsaw that made us complete. Jade looked at me and said, "I can't believe he's ours," as she kissed his head and held him up against her.

I have never felt happiness like it, watching my son being born, holding Jade's hand tight, knowing she would do us proud.

Hours later, in the blink of a second, Jade **died**, just like that. Our whole lives and all we had done to that point was gone, disintegrated into dust. There I was, alone with our new-born Hugo, holding my knees with my hands, just saying to myself quietly, "Keep looking up, put one foot in front of the other, this is all you need to do now, this is your focus."

Time had stopped 100%, and I have never felt the seconds move forward like it. A moment that stays with me forever, the jigsaw had exploded into a million tiny pieces. There I was, looking at Hugo on the hospital bed where I placed him laid next to Jade, crying, while Jade had gone, everything physically and mentally within me **shattered**.

August 2018 – Shock

"The hardest part is not the funeral; it is stepping way beyond this moment. Make your lost loved one proud."

This month was full of **shock**; my eyes were black. I was gone, not knowing what was going on with my body, mind, and soul. Just ensuring I was turning up, putting one foot in front of the other and smiling as much as possible, while deep inside I was in the darkest place no one should face. **Lost, numb,** empty, in disbelief… but knowing I wanted to make Jade proud for her send-off.

Placing my hand on the hearse, never letting go, and on Jade's basket coffin, when Hugo was placed on top of it as a baby, broke me into a million pieces. The jigsaw shattered even more, but I knew I had to find a way, I had to be strong for everyone and be the representation Jade deserved. I just needed to breathe and keep breathing.

August was a month of me getting used to feeding my boy with ease, watching him sleep and being alone with him in our house. I would **cry** every day, which brought me to my knees... breaking me into so many pieces. But to get out of this dark place, I would need to find a way of connecting with Jade. Some nights she would be touching my feet, stroking my face, I didn't know what was happening, but I said "I know you're here, Jade... stay with me... stay with me... please don't leave me... I need you." I've never seen a round of applause after doing a speech on the life of your loved one; this said it all about who we were as a couple and Jade. That day I drank so much without feeling a drop of it, but I knew I couldn't turn to the bottle; this was key.

Finding a routine around Hugo each day was important for me. One positive was the regular support from lots of friends and family every other day. This was important, even though I wasn't really there emotionally, I was there physically, and this was key. I didn't slip further down the black hole.

September 2018 – A very dark place

"I didn't want to be here. It just takes someone to hold your hand, to make you realise you can do this."

Having just dealt with the registration of Jade's passing, I was starting to deal with the administration of her death and wondering: *Why wasn't Jade with us? What had happened? How did this happen? Why did this happen?*

Alongside **deep grief, shock** and **trauma**, my body, in such a short period of time, had taken an almighty spanking: emotionally, spiritually, and physically. Going to Jade's resting place weekly helped. So that is what I did. Every time I looked at Hugo all day, every day since July, I'd had the strongest, heaviest feeling of death. The death of Jade: all the traumatic images in my mind, me not wanting to be on this planet... I prayed deep down and asked deep in my heart for it to go away. When you are sitting on the laptop, writing out your own funeral... step by step,

you are in the darkest of places, trust me. I was alone in this dark place, my head was gone, and I couldn't see a way forward in life.

In a blink, I said yes to a trip away with my brother, and little did I know, this trip would change the course of history and my direction. Digging deep into my soul, saying, "I'm going to come back from this like no man has ever done before."

It was the final evening of the weekend trip away, and it was certainly a boozy one. I was sat there drinking my last beer, and what happened was unbelievable – something that is just crazy when I think about it. A band appeared from nowhere and started to sing 'I will go wherever you will go'.

This was one of *our* songs, I had felt a hand holding mine just before the band appeared. *Was this Jade? Was this a sign?* Either way, it was a surreal moment, and it made me believe and feel deep inside my heart. *I will make you proud. I will do this for you and for our only son Hugo Jaden Hart.* They could have played any song in the world – what are the odds!

October 2018 – Emptiness and disbelief

"Turning the realisation of death and why into preparing for an event in memory is the most powerful thing we can do."

What I was facing this month crumpled me to my knees, the start of **realisation**. **Crying** every day had stopped. *Was something wrong with me?* At the same time, I could feel everything but nothing at all. I wanted to get to the bottom of all this, I knew it would be an **unpredictable** journey, and I had to accept this. Losing someone so close to you: *Jade should be here, helping me feed Hugo, holding him with nothing but unconditional love, kissing him, feeling him, smelling him as a baby, watching him sleep.* All this had gone in the blink of an eye.

I knew though that I needed to **dig deep** into my heart and soul, and after my trip away, I knew two things – running, and bringing people together was important to me, and to others, so that is what happened.

We were all training for the first 10K run, in memory of Jade Hart, and I knew one thing, it was going to be a very powerful, and emotional event. I remember going out for a run in October and having a major panic attack, falling to the ground, but getting back up, putting one foot in front of the other with tears falling in front of me, just saying:

"Keep going, Ric, do Jade proud."

November 2018 – A new focus was on the horizon

"The most powerful thing we can do after loss is to create an event and bring people together to celebrate the life of someone special. We did it in style. Make our lost loved ones proud."

Inside I had to dig deep, still deep in grief, shocked, in disbelief and starting to feel very **angry**. I knew that I needed to make Jade proud, though. I was three months into my loss, and just waking up each day and getting out of bed to feed my boy was an achievement. Not thinking about work, not thinking about finances, not thinking about Jade's case, not thinking about the future, not thinking about others' opinions on what I should be doing and how I should be doing it. Just making sure I was turning up and that Hugo was being fed, was sleeping well and was clean; that was the **focus**.

We did it! What an event, bringing everyone together to run/walk in memory of a very special person. We all had our t-shirts on and ran the Leeds Abbey Dash 10K. I remember looking back with a tear coming down my face at the start of the race, listening to the spa music that we listened to during Jade's pre- and post-birth. I just said to myself:

"Go and run your best time. Just do it."

And I did. I got my 10K PB, and the feeling inside was electrifying, running, my adrenaline, my anxiety hitting the world. Jade was on my mind all the way, and I had tears pouring down from my eyes. What a release – and this is so important. We release as much as we can throughout our deep grief. Trust me, mine was very *heavy*.

December 2018 – I needed to go back

"At times in our lives, we need to go back, back to where it all began, or even started for that matter. Dig deep into the roots of your memories and soul."

I just needed to do this, for me, for Jade, for my heart and soul, digging deep into all those precious **memories**. I had to go back, back to Thailand, where our journey really started, our marriage. I wondered what this was going to do for me, but what was key was that I needed to return. At times through deep grief, we don't need to avoid the **wound**, the **loss**, the memories. We need to stand right in the centre and heart of it all. I needed to feel it, take it in, **breathe**, cry in Thailand. Next time it will be Hugo and Daddy's Thailand Adventures for real! Always hold onto hope and never lose sight of that vision.

I was angry inside, feeling **empty** again. Seeing other families and knowing that most go to bed turning over to their loved one – this screwed me up inside. *Jade should be with me and Hugo* was at the forefront of my mind. Looking at people and saying why Jade? I became lost in my own thoughts. I was looking for someone I couldn't find; she had gone, gone forever. I would go to bed with Hugo by my side and squint my eyes, which were full of tears, and there was Jade, right next to me, within Hugo. For one second, I was like, "Jade, there you are. I can see you."

December 2018, I fell ill. Socialising and being out in public were hard, even going to the local shop. I was starting to become withdrawn, although I had hope through one thing, running. So, I kept on running and releasing my emotions. Christmas was off. It was just another day, but a very heavy and sad one for sure.

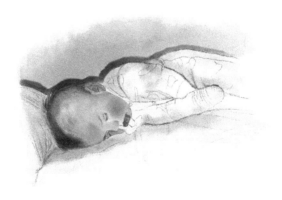

January 2019 — No limits

"My first full year alone... we have to keep pushing for what we are seeking."

The 10K run didn't stop there, that was just the beginning. I knew we had to have something else on the horizon to not only keep me focused but also for others. So, the half marathon was set, March 2019!

"Wow," I said to myself. Finding time to run among all the **chaos** going on, my first year without Jade. Jade's death, my current trauma, and ongoing investigations, my current feelings of anger and of **loneliness** were certainly happening. There's one thing for sure, though, I was starting to find this **calmness** within myself, and it could have gone one way or the other. Either swinging a baseball bat around and abusing people verbally or finding this stillness within my soul, and that's what I did. Some probably thought, *Ric won't say anything*. But never take silence and calmness as weakness, trust me, it's harder.

But I knew as time went on, I would become a very strong man. I had faith in this.

Running was my focus now, nothing else. Taking all my anger out on the streets or alone among the countryside was my answer. Pushing forward to know that I would do 21 km for Jade. Every time I went out running during January, something special was happening while I was out. My whole body would tingle, and I felt like I had electricity within me, this power to do something spectacular for Jade. All these ideas were bouncing around my head. When I looked up to the sky, I saw this H symbol through the clouds. *What was this? A sign, H for Hugo, H for Hart? What was happening to me? Was I losing the plot? Was I going mad? Was I losing my mind?*

February 2019 – My heart was shining bright

"Doing something very special for your lost loved one is key. Hold onto that forever."

February was a very special month. It was the month when Jade and I met, it was the month when we found out we were having a boy, and not only the month, but the exact same day, 14th February – Valentine's Day. It was also the day Jade's stone was laid to **rest** over her grave. What this did for me inside was something else, doing something special for Jade, and this was no ordinary stone. I remember the day so clearly when she was laid to rest. I wanted time alone on my own and was glad everyone respected that. Jade was laid to rest properly in my heart and soul on 14 February 2019 in her hometown, close to her family. Every step and decision I made was selfless, 100% on everything.

Looking back now, I recall standing at Jade's resting place and saying, "I did this for you, I'm doing everything for you. Please keep giving me strength, God, please."

I felt so lit up inside after this day, feeling **proud**. This is what Jade deserved – the best. As I say, this was no normal headstone; it was very special in so many ways.

The moment I got home, I crumpled to the floor. Jade was miles away from me, under the ground, and I was here in our home, all alone with our son. I had to pick myself up again; I had 21 km to run. I said to myself, "Jade, I've fulfilled changing your flowers for the last five to six months. I hope you understand."

March 2019 – Pain and anger at its worst

"When we are forced into a corner in our lives, we can either sink or swim. I decided to take on butterfly!"

This was a month of really believing in my **future** and myself. I didn't have a choice, and potential steps were being taken. I was ready to take on the 21 km half marathon for Jade – a good few turned up, which was amazing. It was so lovely to see everyone and for us all to push ourselves that little bit more for Jade. I was so ill before the run but just got on with it, although having no music as my focus was a major **test**. I clocked the run in around two hours which I was

pleased with; crossing that finishing line was something else inside. On the outside, I may have seemed OK, but never judge a book by its cover, ever. I was in a very dark place again, and there was one thing getting in the way… pride, and my ability to truly open up.

Deep down, I was dying inside. I had officially found out that Jade should still be with us. It was down to decisions made in and around her care, and Jade's death was avoidable.

This shattered me into a thousand pieces, and I had no idea how to scrabble them back together, trying to work out so much in my mind. It was for sure sink or swim but running 21 km stepped me forward with momentum.

I needed to **run away**, I needed to get away, so Vegas it was... I booked my flight late. It was the hardest decision to go away but the best one when I look back now.

April 2019 – Lost, where was I?

"Long and windy roads, in time will eventually lead to beautiful destinations. Just believe."

The feeling inside knowing Jade should be with me, parenting together our only son Hugo, took all my **self-belief** and hope. It was gone... I was starting to have no vision for the future, and just turning up physically was pretty much it. But I needed to focus on the present. As always, new events were on the horizon and parties that I just wasn't up for. I showed up but just wasn't fully there. I was in deep **depression** and angry, low, zapped of life. *Was I starting to lose myself? What was happening with my body?* My nervous system had shattered into a million pieces, just like the jigsaw, and the trauma of my loss felt like it was killing me mentally and psychically.

Trauma for sure is an **injury,** and my body to present had been battered, left, right and centre. Not sleeping; looking after my son 24/7; knowing Jade's death was avoidable; horrific **nightmares** at night, and sobbing in my sleep. I knew this was happening, struggling to wake myself up, but when I did, my pillow was soaking. My body was more sensitive than ever, and I felt everything – but in time, I knew I would turn this into a superpower!

I had to dig deep within my soul and believe I was superhuman. I had this power within me to keep striving forward and believe I was capable of amazing things.

May 2019 – Heavy guilt

*"When something isn't your fault but is so heavy,
I guess it's natural to blame yourself."*

I started to feel very **guilty**, heavy guilt that Jade wasn't here, and she should be. *What could I have done more in the hospital to prevent this? Why didn't we go to Doncaster hospital? Why didn't I ask more questions? Why didn't I challenge the doctors?* 'I could have done something different' was stamped on my forehead. This brought me to an all-time low. I also felt that if I hadn't met Jade, would she still be alive? I was **self-sabotaging** at its worst. I needed to stop.

Every morning when I woke up and looked in the mirror, I just kept on saying to myself, "Ric, you couldn't have done anything, don't do this to yourself."

The one thing I did to deal with my deep grief early on was listening to WhatsApp voice notes, videos, and photos. Around this time, I went back through them all and focused on amazing times, which helped with the guilt.

Being hard on ourselves is part of the **process** and comes in waves. Just breathe and believe in you and what you are doing. I was taking a journey of self-therapy, flipping my trauma into something positive. I felt it, deep within my soul.

June 2019 – Adventures will always help

"Staying in the present is something very powerful. The small things: waking up daily, having our health, being grateful for all we have."

June was a month of adventure; it was my first holiday away with Hugo to Cyprus, and making memories was key for Hugo to look back on. I remember looking at the hill I used to run up when Jade videoed me; she was so proud when I started running more in 2016 when I got the bug.

I remember flying along on the jet ski one day on the seafront. The water was so calm and clear. I felt a level of **freedom**, not being on land, not part of what I was going through. I felt **detached** from my world, my **problems**, and my feelings, and for a minute, I felt better. That was the most powerful minute of so many and much needed.

I just wanted to trek, run for miles, cycle for miles and travel when I could. Life is too short. I was for sure 100% in the present, thinking – *live for today, and do not even worry or wrap yourself up with anything else.*

At the end of June, I cycled to the Lake District, clocking around 150 miles. Again, I wanted to get away from reality, but I was in the present; a very strange place to be in mentally. I was so proud of my cycle trek, another great achievement that stays with me always.

July 2019 – The Jade stone

"Don't stop making our lost loved one proud; just carry that stone with you always. The stone at this moment in time was massive."

It was Hugo's first birthday, and big milestones are always the hardest, especially when Hugo's birthday also holds so much **sadness** with the loss of Jade. Trust me, people, this shit is heavy. I was doing my best, though, to ensure the party went to plan. I was so proud to see Hugo smiling and walking, as he was an early walker at ten-eleven months. I even wrote this down on our goal chart – crazy stuff. I shed a tear for sure that day, a tear of **pain**, which was followed by a tear of love. **Love** for our only son, Hugo Jaden Hart.

I've always been a glass-half-full type of guy, always planning ahead. I wasn't going to let Hugo's birthday and my emotions and others pull me down. We arranged another 10K run for Jade in Leeds the day after, which couldn't have been planned any better. My advice is to do this as much as possible, flip that **negativity** or **emotion**, but not always, as sometimes we need to stand in it all. But what a way to do it! Sunday morning came, it was the day after, and I had hope. I was running for Jade again. What a moment in time, what an achievement. I wasn't going to stop here.

I had sat on my next decision for a year, but it never felt stronger, so I did it – something Jade didn't like… tattoos! But I wanted to do it, imprinting something powerful forever.

August 2019 – "Lost in this world"

"Feeling lost, empty, and angry: these are three bad combinations. We need to keep digging deep and exceeding our own beliefs and expectations. You can do it."

I haven't mentioned this yet, but shortly after the Retford half marathon in March, a good friend of mine ran a full marathon just weeks after – epic stuff! We all need a slight kick up the back side at times, or even some **inspiration** from those around us, and that was mine.

Among all this anger and emptiness, guilt, and feeling so lost in this world, I knew I had a **mission** – I had promised to Jade when she was alive, it was all or nothing, and of course I wasn't sitting back at this point.

I had promised Jade I would run a marathon and train for nine months, as she had grown our boy for nine months and given birth to him. Little did I know I would actually be running this in memory of Jade. I was afraid of the finishing line and what should have been. I started to train properly and knew I only had a few months to get my game face on, as the marathon was in October 2019. I was testing myself, my strength, my ability to break new barriers mentally and physically.

September 2019 – Remove the comfort zone as much as possible

"If we stay in that one place and don't take that step or break new boundaries, we will lose who we are and what we believe we have to offer in this world."

I was thinking about having further tattoos up both arms in memory of Jade and also for Hugo. This was going to be painful but *Go do it* was in my mind. Still to this day, I have no **regrets.** I love them, and this was doing something very special that I will carry with me physically forever.

It was a month before the Yorkshire marathon, and I hadn't run past 28km-ish... shit! Lots of **fear** kicked in, but I knew my mental state would carry me to 42 km, a major test of my inner strength and focus. In the background, I was also dealing with Jade's death and emails from so many official bodies from across the UK. Swamped wasn't the word, along with everything else.

I just focused on that finishing line, **visualising** it. Trust me, running 42km was massive and crazy – but I was doing crazy things, testing my mental state, and breaking some very powerful boundaries. That's what we have to do in life, right? Especially through grief.

October 2019 – The Yorkshire Marathon

"If your dreams or visions don't scare you, they are not big enough! Keep going, test yourself – trust me, you will only grow from it."

The time had come, a monumental moment that underlined my future and **self-belief**. I only had three hours sleep the night before the big run due to nerves. I had not run past 28km, and I was slightly worried. *What if I get an injury? What if I don't finish this for Jade?* I did the sign of the cross at the start as we set off, looked up, and said, "I'm doing it, Jade. I made it to this point; this one is for you 100%."

FINISH - 42 km

What should have been...

Our minds are the most powerful thing we hold. Throughout the whole of the marathon, I just thought of the sixteen-plus years I had with Jade. From start to finish, I vanished into my mind: a very powerful process was happening, and I got to 40 km in around four hours and twenty minutes. The last two kilometres took me about half an hour, but I didn't stop and did a sprint finish. I visualised Jade holding Hugo at the finishing line, nodding at me, sucking her thumb. The reality is, I finished the race, walked to the side gracefully, pounded my chest and said, "You can do anything, Ric Hart – just believe."

The mind is a **powerful** thing. The next morning I had no pain and went and swam 40 lengths... no pain anywhere. Why was this? Because I removed my mind from my body for 4 hours and 50 minutes, something powerful was happening within me.

November 2019 – Low and lonely

"Making new connections and meeting new people is key for our mind, development and finding ourselves again. It's OK to reinvent yourself. It's OK to laugh again."

I had another run to do – the Doncaster 10K, it was a few weeks after my marathon, and I hadn't run at all but clocked a decent time, around 50-ish minutes.

I finished the year on a mega high, all my running, my journey, my thoughts, and feelings – all I was visualising and all my ideas. I was excited to take some very **brave steps**, steps of major **growth**.

I remember dressing Hugo up as an elf and also
Superman that month, a symbol of hope. I had my own
ideas, though, of what that symbol looked like, and was
not letting them go. I had one major **mission** (alongside
a few others) to shout about mine and Jade's life to the
world and to do something special for Hugo.

Was I on track? YES! I wanted to laugh deeply again. I
wanted to just be me but felt I couldn't, not fully, anyway.
So much was holding me back mentally, but I was trying.
I wanted to enter a new universe. I guess I was still
gasping for breath, firefighting, just trying to grind daily.
Making new connections was key to me at this point,
being able to step out of my current circle felt refreshing.

December 2019 – Physical impact

"Our bodies can only take so much; our mental state can crush us physically. Take care of 'you' and never lose sight of that."

It was the second Christmas **alone**, and it felt worse than the first. I fell ill again. My body had dealt with so much over a period of one and a half years, I wanted to disappear. I wanted to go to the other side of the world and just stay there. Behind the scenes, I had my head deeply in and around Jade's care and case; it was heavy and hard. I wanted a break, a break from life, a break from being Daddy, a break from all this pain inside.

Carrying all I had achieved: running; surviving; heavy milestones; Jade's ongoing case, not knowing when the next email would pop up around Jade's care. The shit thing, though, up to this point, was every time I was about to go away or do something special, the heaviest email would drop into my inbox. New information on Jade, new processes that were taking place. We also went to Abu Dhabi this month; it was

Crash and burn

lovely to get away, but when I came back and faced Christmas, I crashed and burned. It needed to happen.

Was I thinking about female company at this point? Of course, I wanted to meet new people, I wanted to socialise, I have so much love to give. Grief is also about having so much love to give, but it doesn't go anywhere; it just gets **bottled up** and becomes a **lead weight** and very emotional. Meeting new people from this point was important to me. I had to find a way to be open, it was about company and new faces for me. On reflection over 2019, was I people-pleasing? Was I saying yes to most things? Was this creating pain inside? More than likely, and yes, the crash and burn in my mind was inevitable.

January 2020 – Deep hope

"When there is more light shone upon hope, we can only smile deep within and say, everything is going to be OK."

After all I had achieved up to this point, it was a mixture of **hope** and the **unknown**, and that **scared** me. It still does, I guess, but I had more hope inside, more belief, and I felt this was my year to do something amazing. I didn't know what that was or looked like, but I had a good feeling inside. We must hold onto that and never let it go, ever. Looking back, I had also stopped changing Jade's flowers on the PUPY sign, which I had been doing every two weeks for up to six months this time last year, from August 2018-February 2019. It was a process I needed to go through, but I had to **let go** of that, breaking it all up and stepping forward and also in my mind.

I was also finding it hard to express all my feelings to most people around me but looking back now, that is fine. *How could I express in clear, constructive words what was happening in my mind? I couldn't. Did I find it hard to connect to most? Yes. Did I have that go-to person/people, though, when I needed to vent or express?* Yes, and thank God for that. Cherish those people; they are important to you. What I did know was that I needed to meet new people; make new connections. I had lots of anger deep inside at the start of 2020, with many dark thoughts still lingering around my mind. I also had a counsellor I was visiting back and forth in the latter part of 2019, but that process was cut short. While venting had helped, I needed to walk away from that to explore self-therapy. What this looked like, though, was the question?

February 2020 – Test of strength

"At times, we need to look back, to test our strength and measure where we are at; it's just part of our growth."

February was such a special month, especially the 14th, as it was the date Jade and I met; the date we found out we were having a boy, and when Jade's headstone was laid to rest on her grave, and it also had a future meaning which I will write about later in this book.

February was also a month for me to look back at some very horrific images, images that snapped my spine, in 2018, and 2019. This was how I found a way to **grow**, found a way to assess where I was at, how I was feeling. While my spine didn't snap, I still had this **gut-wrenching** feeling with so much emotion. It felt that little bit better. It  was not all about just looking at the lovely images; sometimes, not always, we need to look at the hard ones. It's our test. I was testing my **strength** at this point on all I had achieved.

What was on the horizon? Nothing much, really; it felt like something strange was in the air.

Did I believe in love after love? Did I have hope I would find someone? Is there such a thing as a second chapter, a new soul mate? Is there such a thing as finding that exciting young love again? I believed...

Hugo was just over one and a half years old. Life was tough, but with my loss: the heaviness; Jade's ongoing case; grief and trauma, having hope was key. I always kept hold of it. What was important, though, was going with my gut – we all know the gut feeling, but mine didn't feel the same. *Was this my grief? Was this my body taking a battering over the last 18 months? Was this confusion, or was I forcing processes?* It all became very clear throughout my story, shared further within this book.

I did however manage to go and visit Jade's engraving on the 'Heart of Steel' at Meadowhall in Sheffield. This is where Jade used to work and where her career had really started – a very special moment which was created by Jade's Nana.

March 2020 – Ten steps backwards

"When that moment happens, and we go backwards mentally into that dark place, losing all hope, we just need to say to ourselves, there is only one way, and that's up."

I was at the point of needing to socialise more, smile and not feel guilty. To dance and **forget** about this horrible world and circumstances I was in – I had hope. That all shattered and fell to pieces. Everything that I had done and placed myself within mentally crashed and burned. We were hit with a pandemic, Covid-19 struck the world, and it certainly struck me. The pane of glass had shattered into a million pieces again. I was all alone with Hugo at twenty-one months old for a period of 12 weeks. Drained, low, depressed, grieving, **craving affection**, lost again. I had to just wake up daily, be present, breathe, be grateful and start to believe in my mind and all my ideas and what I was capable of.

Give me strength...

Everything: my routine; structure; **mindset; attitude;** focus; grief; hope; **determination; motivation** and drive had all altered. I needed to realign and accept a new set of processes, locked up with my boy. This broke me and took me back into my deep grief. Looking after a 22-month-old toddler is tough enough in lockdown, but I had everything else on top of me. I felt very low, sad, and lost. All hope had gone; it dissolved into thin air just like that. Grief and trauma can physically paralyse you. I look back now and for so long, just getting out of bed was an achievement. Now ask yourself, could you get through 12 weeks alone and locked up with a twenty-two-month-old? Every day, doing everything, trying to catch your breath, **firefighting,** while coping with my emotions and mental state. Trust me, guys, it was another huge challenge that I faced.

April 2020 – The light bulb moment

"At times, we need to realign, adjust, accept the present moment, but see it as a blessing. My blessing was upon me."

Even though I was faced with extremely **hard times** in lockdown, I was also presented with a blessing, a blessing of me and my son bonding even more. With time alone, away from everyone and the world. We were going for country walks and bike rides in the fresh air. The sun was beaming, and that made me smile. I had this image of creating a spa garden. *What did this look like?* I thought, and so I planned it in my mind.

One day I woke up in April, and all my ideas from running were coming so strong to me, it was unreal. Like someone or something saying, just do it, **take that step**.

So, I did, I started writing 2000 words every morning before Hugo woke about mine and Jade's life. I also designed a children's book, sketching out image ideas and some poetry to go with it. I was taking major steps forward; this was my focus. The light started to shine bright in my heart, a glimpse of hope came back. I was so excited and had this huge vision going forward. I mapped it all out in my mind and went for it with all my heart.

May 2020 – A new book author was on the horizon

"Creativity will save us, allow us to grow, give us that satisfaction inside. If we don't take that step, we will never know."

As I started to write, out came the life of me and Jade, and I really got into it. I said, "This is a book, the book of our lives." The one thing I promised I would do for Jade, which was share our lives and story to the world. I was excited, the first real feeling of **excitement** in my life, two years after Jade's passing. Just like that! I had created a children's book – the poetry was done; the flow and images were sketched and kind of on point. *Hugo and Daddy's Night-time Adventures* was born from just some paper and a pencil.

lockdown writing

The pandemic stopped my running – my outlet, which was hard for me mentally. I had to shift from all the physical to a mental outlet, and it was working – although I stacked a few pounds back on, *lol*. It was also a time when we were allowed our first meet-up with family. Deep down, I was still 'me,' inviting hugs all round, but I guess we just had to respect other people's **attitudes**. I was also so **happy** I had found my illustrator for the children's books and my publisher – the **ideas** and vision were happening.

June 2020 – Feeling proud inside

"When we believe deep in our hearts we are placed on this planet for a reason, it is a great step forward mentally. Just visualise, believe, and you will achieve, find your why and purpose and hold onto that."

The spa garden was coming along nicely. I was starting to *focus* more on me and my *self-care*. I guess it was a journey exactly how I wanted it. Hugo's children's book was in production with my illustrator, and the inflatable hot tub was set up. I could find **relaxation** on evenings with a cold beer when Hugo was asleep; pure bliss came to mind.

I needed to focus on me, I needed to provide as much self-care as possible, and I accepted this as something that must be maintained throughout my life. My body had been destroyed at all angles, and I needed to keep looking after my wellbeing. "Health is wealth, people!" I've always said this through my life. What are we doing at the minute to improve or create a better version of us, mentally and physically? This was at the forefront of my mind, staying alive and well for as long as possible. I self-taught myself the guitar, which I really enjoyed, learning some meaningful parts of songs, which I still remember now. Learning some of the chords broke me inside, but I felt slight growth, just an ounce, and I cried happy tears. Our subconscious is powerful!

I also set up something very special, a website
www.jadehartpupylove.co.uk.

The world started to open back up properly. I really wanted to meet someone. *Was I ready?* When we understand what we need and what we want and distinguish action between the two, it is a powerful place to be.

I knew one thing; I was still so lonely inside, and it became painful. I did feel very vulnerable throughout the summer of 2020 with all that I had lost; gone through; lockdown; my writing, and my feelings. My body was being reborn again, or it certainly felt that way. While quite vulnerable, it also felt like a combination of emotions such as *anxiety, adrenaline,* and something unknown – all together.

July 2020 – I didn't want any part of any of this!

"When we have a serious responsibility to manage, just take that first step and have a vision. A new normal takes time, deep breaths every morning."

Jade's care was substandard on so many levels, among so many decisions, one after the other, up to the point of birth and post-birth. This broke me – from finding this out officially in February 2019 and onwards. Learning more as time went on, I was living with this **heavy burden** for nearly one and a half years. I guess it is a life sentence to a certain degree.

I was faced with a financial settlement to handle as a result in the heart of the lockdown, but all I knew was that Jade should still be here. I remember pacing around my house the following day, dealing with something that felt heavier than the world. My t-shirt had changed colour from sweat as, through my own mind, I had got my heart rate pounding. *What do I do? How do I deal with this?* But most importantly, I had a **plan**. We are either spending, saving, or investing in this world. I decided to have a plan to start to create a major investment.

My plan was to build 'generation wealth'. It certainly wasn't about handing major cheques out to everyone, which is what, more than likely, some thought just crazy... I was on a journey of building: to add value over the next two generations, throughout my life, and also Hugo's family's life when I'm long gone, alongside building an income to create upkeep of my life, replacing where the household income was, and what was lost, while being full time to Hugo. Some might say I'm not humble, laughable really. I knew it would take time, but I had a *vision*. I do know one thing, though, I'm a very kind person and always have been. It's an eye-opener when money comes into the fold, as over time, you start to see whose skin it gets under and who just wants you to be genuinely happy regardless of decision-making, and this stands out like a sore thumb.

What we truly deserved and needed was Jade with us, as a family, but that had shattered. I've got a good head on my shoulders, and as I look back now, I've made some amazing decisions for mine and Hugo's life, and we will find as much happiness going forward as we deserve, 100%! Also, choose wisely what you share with people; those you think you can trust may just turn out to be untrustworthy. Finding that inner circle is key, but that is a journey in itself. Glide through it, learn from it. The smaller the circle, the better, be OK with that. Not everyone needs to know your business, and not everything needs an explanation.

Throwing this book out to the universe and sharing my journey helps me. This isn't me exposing all my decision-making but simply releasing my current life and reality as a snap shot to the world; lifting a lead weight off my shoulders, writing and sharing helps. Not everyone will get this, though all book authors will.

Do what you want that makes you happy, live for today, build for the future in the best way you can with the resources you have. As I look back upon the summer of 2020, I'm proud of my decisions, as most of them were solid, creating a sound structure for both mine and Hugo's life. I guess the very small per cent I had fun with was cars – there was nothing else to enjoy in the pandemic, so why not? – We only live once! And the bottom line is they were just cars… nothing else... I'm so glad I'm at a point in my life now where this doesn't weigh me down anymore. It means I am getting on with my life, making decisions, not feeling guilty, alongside being very savvy.

August 2020 – Craving for affection but lost at the same time

"At times, we feel we need someone when we have been alone for so long. Craving someone, that connection, but in reality, all we need to do is find ourselves and create self-love."

As I look back now at August 2020, a little over two years since Jade died – I was lonely and lost. Lost within myself and who I was, and felt I needed to find someone. It's natural, I guess, when in grief, we have so much love to give. I felt **vulnerable.** All this as a combo, stepping out, meeting new people is not good, but you have to take that step to see what it feels like. Get out of your **comfort zone** as much as you can, but it is OK to retreat. Just don't stay there forever.

Going with my gut, but was my body and mind actually plugged in? Was I blaming my grief for not 'feeling' or being confused by my gut?

It was an explosion of emotions. I felt like I was on the 'Pepsi Max' ride in Blackpool!

Hugo and Daddy's Night-time Adventures was all set, and the illustrations were done. It was with the publishers, ready to publish for October 2020, and I was about to officially become a book author. The fire inside of me lit up, and I felt alive again, proud, excited. I decided to give back, so I placed *Night-time Adventures* with the national charity Cruse Bereavement – In my mind, I just saw, NON-PROFIT BOOK AUTHOR, I was doing something truly powerful within myself.

Evening therapy

September 2020 – I wasn't thinking straight – it happens!

"Making bad decisions, doing silly things – it's part of the journey! Make the decisions, learn from them, but accepting a new normal takes time."

As I look back at this month, I was still lost, **confused** among my new set of circumstances. I woke up one day and bought a 2000-plate old Fiesta 1.2L for £900. Looking back now, what was I doing? I don't think I was accepting my current circumstances. I didn't really want any part of any of it, but as I mentioned, I had a plan. I didn't have the car long, only a few months and then gave it away – a funny moment, really. We all do **crazy** things, and this was one of mine. The one positive is that it took me back to when I was 17 in my brother's Fiesta and cruising to sixth form. That was nice to go back to in my mind. If Hugo could talk properly back then, I know one thing, he would be calling me Mr Bean and laughing his head off.

"Daddy, I don't like this car!" would have come to mind!

Another huge positive at this point was that my property business was emerging from decisions made in 2019 and spring 2020. I had huge growth ideas going forward with this. I remember I was completing on some properties in 2019 and early 2020, and the estate agents said that it was a gamble, as they didn't know where the market would go. For me, though, it was a long-term investment. Looking back now, wow!

Some great decisions on some solid properties, with huge growth within. I had two major focuses, my book author journey and building a property empire to provide an income for my life and also the future. Again, my decision-making was focused on 'generational wealth'. I was also in the process of building my home gym, another vision to improve my physical and mental health.

October 2020 – Was I finding my purpose? My 'why' was right beside me

"Holidays are always going to be hard, but you have just got to grind and hope that it gets better as time goes on. Trust me, it does."

Me and Hugo went off to Greece this month for a break away with family, but this turned out to be extremely **challenging.** My head was a shed; I had dealt with so much mentally throughout the year, with lockdown, loneliness, deep grief, and Jade's case. The human body can only take so much. The one thing that was allowing me to have hope was the launch of my debut children's bereavement book. The holiday was challenging as it was so hard dealing with Hugo at only 27 months. In life, we've got to do what we have to do – I went back to the room most evenings because I couldn't deal with any more paddies and crying. Hugo crying took me back to my own trauma. I have no idea how I got through my darkest days with my deep trauma attached to a baby crying, as it was happening all day, every day. I had to do what was best for my heart and soul.

During the final days on holiday, I launched my children's book. I made a video to share the pre-order launch while I was on the beach, and I was so excited for so many reasons – the fire was burning bright inside. In short, *Hugo and Daddy's Night-time Adventures* did so well, based on the mass volume of orders. It got to number two on the best sellers list for one of its book categories. It held best rankings four weeks after launch and was 2nd, 5th, and 7th for all three book categories. I felt something deep within my soul. *You're doing it, Ric, making Jade proud, doing something different and supporting Hugo. Being creative and giving back in a special way and healing your soul.*

I had so much **support** from my inner and outer circle and so many others, it was unreal. Social media ballooned, the local press got hold of my debut book, and I also spoke on radio stations. This was just the start of a very special and beautiful journey for me, a very deep, meaningful project to help me and hopefully so many out there. *Wow* just came to mind – *I'm officially a book author, the guy who can't even write or read well and is rubbish at English literature!* It just shows, if we want to do something deep down, which holds meaning and purpose, we can make it happen.

November 2020 – We only live once, do what makes you happy or at least have a go

"Grief is like a lifelong degree, where we get tested at certain points. You will never have the answers in the present, but experience will show you them."

Hugo and Daddy's Night-time Adventures hit the media, which was lovely to see. When you bring out a book, trust me, you shout as far and as wide as possible – but I knew this was a **journey**. I woke up one morning and thought, *I'm going to go and buy my dream car, a BMW i8. Why not?* I could, and life is too short, not boasting or showing off just my reality.

There was nothing really to look forward to due to lockdown, and the only enjoyment I could get was out on the roads, so why bloody not! The reality was, when I picked it up, I felt empty, I felt nothing; it was just a car to me. Just a piece of metal, it felt far from a dream, but the reality was I could die tomorrow, so why bloody not. I was on a rocky road of accepting a new normal and a different set of circumstances in relation to decision-making.

I will say something, though, looking back, I never changed as a person ever. Those closest to me know this, I guess it was people's attitudes towards my new decision-making which I understood would be hard, but that really wasn't mine to take on. I had lost everything. We make decisions, live, learn and grow through grief, but life just looks clearer for sure over time.

Self-care was so important to me at this point, so I decided to invest in a proper hot tub. Looking back now it was the best thing I've bought. This was epic for post-workouts and joint support and just relaxation. I was building something very beautiful at home, my gym and my spa garden. When we have the ability to invest in us, just do it. Again, people, **health is wealth**. The Christmas tree was up early so we could have a longer Christmas feeling, and it felt better this year.

December 2020 – On reflection, if you don't feel it straight away, walk away

"If you don't feel it straight away, don't act on it. Something that I live by now with so much power."

The building of the indoor gym was making progress, and *Hugo and Daddy's Night-time Adventures* did amazingly in its first two months from launch. Eight weeks later, it had made about £8,000 in gross book sales, which was phenomenal, and after costs to the publishers and printing, etc., it left just under £1,300, which is still amazing. This was passed on to the charity Cruse Bereavement Care, and what this did for me inside was amazing the book also got the 2nd best seller on Amazon for weeks, sitting in the top 20 for a good month or so. Phenomenal I was executing everything I had planned in my mind. *Pupy Love* was also with the editors and publishers, ready for an early 2021 publishing date. Let's not forget I'm a non-profit book author, and I didn't even cover my costs, but those costs were the start of self-therapy at its best. The chosen charity for *Pupy Love*'s profits was WAY: Widowed and Young, my **fire inside** in relation to my book journey was shining bright.

It was the next lockdown – *Not another one*, I said to myself. But I had so many ideas flying in my mind, and one morning I sat at the dining table, and a few hours later, *Hugo and Daddy's Thailand Adventures* was born. A beautiful projection of the steps I would take with Hugo, in all the amazing places in Thailand.

I kept seeing this 'H' symbol; it was so strong in my mind – it appeared for *Night-Time Adventures* and *Thailand Adventures* and when I was out running. *What was this?* I knew straight away: it was Hugo's superhero sign, and a symbol of the hope and strength I had shown through my journey, but mainly for Hugo. I was a very busy author, deep in the emotions of it all for Hugo, for Jade's legacy, and for my heart. Just like that, *Hugo and Daddy's Superhero Adventures* emerged – I will share more on this later in the book. I was acting on everything, and my **creativity** was pouring out. I was doing my author journey in lockdown style, with long hair nearly hitting my shoulders and a grisly beard! But I was taking action on every idea, literally everything.

Ric's Rules:

1. Follow your dreams
2. Follow your passion
3. Give something back
4. Choose love

January 2021 – A major step forward in my mind

"Doing something very special and sharing it to the world will do wonders for your heart and soul. Never underestimate grief, though. At times, we think we can beat it, but, oh no, this stays with you forever."

This was a very special month and an amazing start to the new year. I was collating all the images and **memories** I had received from those closest to Jade from 2020, for the back of the book. Such a lovely touch. I appreciate so many amazing memories shared, respect to so many doing this for Jade. I was also creating the videos and content ready to launch the publication of *Pupy Love*. The date was set – 14 February 2021, a no-brainer of a date!

This was a crazy month, so many mixed emotions. Did I want someone special in my life? A special companion, yes? Was I getting this gut feeling as I look back now? No... Was I blaming my grief? Yes. *Give things time, Ric,* I said. Again, looking back now, if you do not have that excited gut feeling inside, walk away. A very confusing state of mind with so much going on and very difficult to explain, don't force anything on this planet, and allow your body to recover and come back.

Also, at the end of this month, I drove to Doncaster and Bassetlaw Teaching Hospital and parked at the same point where we parked on the day when Jade was going in to be induced. I stood outside the hospital, looking straight into the ICU window from the road and saw myself where I was in July 2018, recalling what I said to myself, "Make Jade proud." It was a moment where I was looking at my past self, but also, perhaps I was seeing my future self? A surreal moment.

Time to step forward?

February 2021 – Sharing our lives with the world

"When we have a strong vision and goal, never let it go, never lose sight of it; it all depends how much we want it. I made a promise to someone who is no longer here; execute it in the best way."

I can't believe I did it, *Pupy Love*, the story of our lives, was published 14 February 2021, with proceeds going to the charity WAY – Widowed and Young. I couldn't have been prouder on a very special day for tons of reasons. I achieved something very special and **powerful** at the same time. I stopped and pinched myself. *OMG, Ric, this is your second published book!* I was providing **self-therapy**, I was growing through my grief, my fire inside was shining bright.

I was so wrapped up in taking action on my ideas, I had two more books moving through the illustrations stage and aiming for the summer to publish them both. *Thailand* and *Superhero Adventures* were both done. Not only going back to Thailand for a glimpse in December 2018 but creating Hugo's second children's book and visualising this through art was **healing** my soul. I was pulling myself out of this very dark place through my own steps and decisions, and trust me, folks, there is nothing more powerful. I decided at this point that my next books would be placed with a local charity, The Children's Bereavement Centre in Newark.

March 2021 – New directions, new steps

"Craving normality is fine, but for who, is the question? We can only live and learn through that and work everything out after our decision is made. There is a lesson and blessing in every decision we make in life, which pushes us to accept a new normal.*"*

Throughout my journey so far: nearly three years into the loss of Jade, all I had done, my actions taken, my sacrifices, being kind and considerate, had mostly been selfless, deep within my soul. This was the point when I was about to take a journey through **stepping forward,** and these were **big steps**. There should be no judgment on stepping forward in your life from others, just support and understanding. I say if you have nothing positive to say, say nothing at all, and if you are negative and voice it, it will more than likely come back and bite you on the arse. *Was I putting myself first, though? Or was I craving normality for my son? His schooling, the next few years?*

Hugo was always the priority. I had been dealing with a unique and tragic set of circumstances that had **consequences** that I was trying my best to work with. I was on the verge of sacrificing so much, emotionally, financially, physically – the lot. All to create potential normality for my son and his schooling, his next few years, and mine. This was at the forefront of my mind, and hopefully an ounce of happiness for me. I look back now on so much, some may think I wasn't being humble, but if this isn't being humble, I don't know what is. I chose to find some form of normality again or what I thought was normality. It was very much about Hugo's future at the time and what I thought he needed around him first and foremost, it was far from about the pound signs.

April 2021 – Putting so many first, still

"Choices, decisions all have positive and negative consequences. All you can do is keep going, fall forward, grow forward."

Looking back now, wow, what an incredible month of involving others, bringing so many into my journey. My decision-making was still selfless – how did I feel about all of this? I wanted a fresh start at life, but looking back now, it's very important we make decisions for us and ensure it's what we want for us, and us only. I was the nucleus for Hugo, and the better version I was of myself, the better version Hugo would be. I think I lost sight of this; I was too focused on what he needed around him, and all he needed was the best version of his dad. It takes time to accept a new normal, and at times we **crave normality** or try to take that step into it. The reality is, there is nothing normal about what had happened to me and Hugo, Jade wasn't just another death; this held a level of rarity with a different set of circumstances. But… we can't stay in the same place forever, we **step forward**, we live and learn.

One positive for my hygiene was I cut my hair! Looking back, it took from February 2020 to April 2021 to grow my hair from short to hitting my shoulders – madness really. All the emotions my mind and body had gone through linked to my long hair were incredible.

Just like that, it was snipped off, and it felt like the whole of 2020 had just dropped off my shoulders too. I was sat in 2021 with a new set of circumstances, falling forward, stepping forward, making decisions, and watching all this prevail.

May 2021 – Craving a new life

"Sometimes in life, certainly after grief, loss, or adversity, it's hard to take that leap of faith, the unknown. But if we don't jump, we will never know, we will never learn, we will never grow."

I had made a massive decision to step forward into a new life; my aims were selfless, bar some potential happiness for me. I guess when you can make big decisions in life, why not? – We all make decisions which hold negative and positive **consequences.** We have to stand firm and do what we **believe** is right at the time. I had Hugo massively on my mind, and I recall pretty much the first day of stepping forward. At that moment, I wondered – *What have I done?* My soul was erupting with anxiety and stress when it should have been a champagne moment for sure. The home gym at Swallows Nest had just finished, that was approximately a 7K project, and I think I got to use the gym once... "Wow, that's some gym pass, lol."

The gym was built, but I was off...

73

The gym flooring had just gone down, the walls had been skimmed, but I was off to pastures new!

Having written *Pupy Love*, going through the rollercoaster of this from April 2020 up to present, and releasing the book, I had this **acceptance** feeling inside. I felt I had beaten all my darkest of days. I look back now, and I did beat deep grief. I was also ready to step forward with as much positivity and momentum for Hugo and myself as possible. Looking back now in 2022, it doesn't happen like that; I believe you can beat deep grief, but not grief. I was never going to let go of Jade: she is Hugo's birth mother and always will be. She remains with us both for the rest of our lives, in our own way, you can't just shut that out, and I didn't want that anyway. I had also received the first book for *Hugo and Daddy's Thailand Adventures*, I was so excited for Hugo, and my creativity and ideas were definitely not going to stop for nobody.

As I looked back through my wing mirror... I said, "Goodbye Swallows Nest," with a tear coming down my face... but was it a goodbye forever?

June 2021 – My creative point at its peak

"Having a vision is key. Ensure you are doing it for the right reasons, go with your gut, make decisions; it will either be a blessing or a lesson."

Wow, at this point on my journey, I was in a totally different dimension. Stepping forward, **taking chances**, involving so many in special projects, with this beautiful projection of creating a new world for Hugo and myself. On reflection, when we start to make decisions for ourselves, or what we think is right for us at the time, we learn a lot about others and their feelings based on their actions/words and also our own. I was doing my best to survive through an ordeal no one should ever have to face. Sometimes life is trying to teach you something or provide you with a beautiful blessing. Find the blessing

in everything I say but observe that in stepping forward, you may need to **navigate** a tricky landscape of the emotions of those around you alongside you trying to find happiness. *Hugo and Daddy's Thailand Adventures* was published on 24 June 2021, and I couldn't have been more excited. I was taking a very special journey for us both through my grief.

It was a beautiful projection of the steps I took with Jade, of having hope that one day I would take Hugo with me to all the beautiful islands to share some special moments with him, as an amazing memory of a very special time and place, deep within my heart. This book didn't do as well as the first – support around me for this project dissolved, but that was OK. My book journey wasn't, and isn't, about fame or being a best seller, or even feeling the need for everyone to get behind my book journey. It was about what it did for me inside. The books are very niche: good self-therapy, providing my heart and soul with so much love for Hugo, and a legacy to Jade. I was proud.

July 2021 – Bringing everyone together again!

"Life is an eye-opener; when this happens, your world starts to look much clearer."

A very special month for Hugo, his third and yet his first proper birthday celebration. I threw a massive party and was very excited for him. He deserved the best after the last two years, so I went all out, making it very special and inviting family and close friends. Bearing in mind Covid, we managed a big bash anyway – I saw the bigger picture, and everyone needed to be invited, within the covid rules anyway. Yes, it was a bells and whistles event, but bricks, mortar and tangibles didn't change me, My decision-making affected many, but I was still me, growing, learning, and

striving forward. Life was just looking clearer and clearer, and I was on this journey of finding my way to grow and gain even more **clarity.**

I created **www.hartshero.co.uk** with Hugo's own H symbol, which I trademarked, also his own merchandise page and some video content too. I loved our H symbol and decided to have it tattooed on my arm; it looks epic! H for Hope, H for Hugo Hart, H for Hart's Hero, which is what Hugo is called in the book, as his own superhero. What kid wouldn't want to be a superhero! I was bringing this all to life for Hugo, a projection of when he starts school: finding strength, confidence and hope in all he does. My head at this point was honestly a shed. I had major doubts about the recent changes, feeling lost and praying things would get better in my mind. I just kept on saying, "Give it time, Ric." I was sacrificing so much and compromising so much it was unreal, some things in life, looking back now, cannot be compromised. We live and *learn*.

August 2021 – Hart's Hero was born!

"When so much is going on, and we are wrapped up among it all, all we need to do is strip it all down. Keep being true to yourself, keep being true to your feelings."

Looking back, this was a **rollercoaster** of a month emotionally and behind the scenes in my life. All I said to myself again was, *What have I done?*

Jade's birthday was also on the horizon, and Hugo's superhero book was ready to be launched, with so much to do in terms of marketing and content.

I had such a busy summer but nothing was changing how I was feeling. I guess we can only mask things for so long before it all crashes and burns. At this point, I was doubting my present moment, and the crash and burn was inevitable. Life was crazy, but I knew in my heart this wasn't forever.

One positive was the publication of Hugo's third children's book, *Hugo and Daddy's Superhero Adventures*, which represented the **strength** I had through my darkest of days. The character Hart's Hero for Hugo is a projection of him as a five to six-year-old at school, being confident, eating well and being the best boy he can be at school. As I write this, I think he's smashing it, and he does love his book, picking it up at random times. Although he is writing his name backwards, so I guess I will have to keep an eye on that one going forward. I was also very excited to launch my video on hartshero.co.uk, sharing the vision and ideas behind it all. I still believe this book journey and our symbol of Hope will always keep finding new homes and children out there. Again the profits from this book were given to the Children's Bereavement Centre alongside the *Thailand* book.

September 2021 – Hugo starts nursery school

"Being in the best place possible for your own sanity, heart, and soul. It's not a need; it's a must, regardless of decisions made and circumstances."

Hugo was starting his new nursery at school, and it was a huge step for us both, and this was my priority; he looked so beautiful and excited. I was also wrapped up in what had been a three-month full refurbishment. The book frames were being nailed to the walls, the carpets were down, and the new log burner was installed.

Where was my head? Well, it wasn't where I was... Deep down within my soul, I needed to go back, realign. My decisions and steps in 2021 had been to create happiness for me and Hugo, but I listened, watched, and did enough observing for a lifetime to realise I needed to take a step back. It was going to be one of the hardest steps and processes among so much going on, but my name is Ric Hart, and there's one thing I have shown on my journey: massive inner strength, creativity, and now it was time to show bravery and be true to me.

I was doing something very special, juggling many projects bringing so many into it. Again, as a non-profit book author, putting others first, helping and supporting and aiming to inspire. While my decisions were pretty much selfless, I needed to face reality. I needed to be honest with myself, I needed to listen to my gut. My God, it was working. I've never felt it scream so loud inside, like a volcano erupting.  You can never mask your true feelings; they will always surface at some point.

October 2021 – Engraving our symbol forever

"In Life, at times, we need to follow our gut, be true to ourselves, and mark 'us' as the main priority. If we don't, 100% we will lose who we are and the best version of who we can be, regardless of circumstance."

This month I decided to follow this beautiful journey I was on with my tattoos and decided to get Hugo's H symbol stamped on my forearm. It was a random decision but felt right, and something really cool as an addition to my tattoos for Hugo on my left arm. Something I will always look upon. And Hugo, even now, he still loves it, and he keeps saying, "Daddy, I want one." *Lol.*

I remember sitting there in the chair at the tattoo place, and it felt like I was in the process of just doing 'me' and 'me' only. Ready to show some bravery throughout my life. It was an imprint and the final straw, that little voice saying... *Do what's best for you, Ric. You need to be 100% happy. You deserve to be 100% happy.* H for hope.

I also had an idea constantly ringing in my head around 'Real with Ric', a thought I kept visualising. Talking out on Instagram, sharing my circumstances.

Jade's case was still progressing, waiting for confirmation of when the inquest would be in early 2022. The potential criminal investigations had ended in late 2020, and various bodies in the UK were still pending in relation to Jade's circumstances. I had my own theories behind all this, and it wasn't good – Do we live in a failed and corrupt system? Again, we have a choice in life, and I could have just sat like a couch potato and let depression and anger swamp my life, not a chance. All I wanted and needed around me was true understanding, compassion, empathy, and kindness. I knew one thing, though, over the next six months I was going to need to be in the best place possible: mentally, physically, and emotionally. This was 100% a must, and I needed to be true to myself. In life, we make mistakes, but as long as we learn from them, it becomes a lesson, making you stronger, braver, and wiser on this planet.

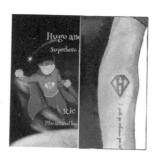

November 2021 – Facing the truth deep within my heart and soul

"In life at times, we are faced with serious challenges, but I guarantee this, if you don't face them, be true to yourself, and fall forward, you will never grow in this life."

This was a month of **acceptance**; of hard decisions; of showing massive **bravery**; of being true to myself; of taking **action**; of facing the music. Christmas was just around the corner, and the end of the year. Nothing mattered, nothing, other than going back, realigning, restructuring my life for me and my happiness. All I needed to do was be true to myself, accept, make decisions for me, and the rest would sort itself out. Hugo and Daddy were ready to march on. I held my head high, stood tall, and did what was best for me, nobody else, just me.

Where was my head, though? Was I unstable? NO! *Was I having a breakdown?* NO! Life never looked clearer; my clarity was very good. I knew who I was, what was important to me, what I was willing to accept and move forward with and what I wasn't. I knew this was going to be my journey for now and the next few months.

We live and learn in life, don't we? And 2021 was very much a lesson for me, but also a blessing. Having watched, listened and observed for so long, I knew there was only one thing to do after waking up one morning at 3am with Hugo beside me. I said to myself, "I'm going back, back to our home, Swallows Nest, back to Ric's sanctuary." With a whole new mindset. WOW – I had a vision, and I've never felt warmth and happiness like it.

I was back!

Running Doncaster 10K 2021!

December 2021 – Feelings of failure, loss, and guilt

"In life, through loss and adversity, it's OK to crash and burn, it's OK to make mistakes, it's just part of your journey of growth and of clarity. It's OK to lose yourself, but finding 'you' again, this is growth. Trust me, you're on the right path. Realising what you don't want and what cannot be compromised is a powerful place to be."

I was somewhere I didn't want to be, but I had to ride this storm out, and putting the Christmas tree up was hard. It was a 12-footer with all the trimmings, yet deep down, it was harrowing, but it was for my boy, Hugo.

Making Christmas feel as special as possible for him – I smashed it. Piggybacking him down the stairs alone on Christmas Day, so much excitement to see if Santa had been. The air didn't smell the same, and my four walls didn't look the same – I was ready to plan my exit. Leaving so much behind, while the bricks and mortar meant nothing, this was heavy. But I had to deal with it, walk away, having sacrificed so much emotionally and financially. I was ready to realign on this planet for me, and me only.

My clarity had never been stronger. I wasn't putting up with rubbish or negativity anymore from anyone. I was ready to take even braver steps, steps towards being true and real to me.

Christmas was special for Hugo

All I was planning was my next move. We can mask or try to cover troubles in our life 'til the fat lady sings', but we always need to be true to ourselves and our feelings. I look back, and to this moment, most, if not all, of my decisions were selfless, but now it was about me, 100%, and nobody else. "Hugo will be fine," I kept on saying to myself, and he is. As I write this now, we are in a great place together, both of us, a million times over.

New Year's Eve struck. I had let go of anything attached to me. I danced in the kitchen with a beer, then headed out for a night out on the tiles with a friend. My mood board was written, and goals set for 2022.

My God, it was going to be a year of massive growth for me and massive challenges, but finding me again, realigning, being true to myself and putting me first. Trust me, this was hard. I had to consider Hugo and the surrounding circumstances, but in life we must do this post-trauma and grief.

You will know when the time is right to press the button on you and you only – it's a must. 2022 was about me, my decisions, my growth, because I deserved to be in the best place possible, 100%.

January 2022 – Hugo and Daddy's New Adventures

"Make decisions; ride the train of life; be true to your feelings; stay strong; remove negativity, focus only on where you're heading. The most important thing is to make sure YOU are driving. People leave, people get pushed, new people enter – embrace it and accept it."

This year was about making solid decisions and standing by what was right. Being true to me and not putting up with any shit off anyone. Lots was happening – focusing on a new life direction, a new book for Hugo. Hugo was taken out of the local nursery; we (Hugo and Daddy) were ready to jump back on that rocket! *Get me the hell outta here* was in my mind. Again, we live and learn, and I needed to go through this process; it was paramount to my journey.

I also had Jade's inquest hearing, and I felt scared, nervous, anxious, and didn't know what to expect. Finally, some answers and clarity came to mind, or so I hoped. I had been waiting nearly four years for this. The weight on my back had been so heavy it felt like I was holding the world up with one arm. I was about to turn Hugo's routine upside down, walking away from the current house, leaving it empty, a substantial sum of money. To return to mine and Jade's old home, Swallows Nest.

I was dealing with Jade's inquest and so much more in the background – it was unreal, doing most of this alone, which was my choice. I remember my body felt like I was back in survival mode as if I had fought 12 rounds of boxing every day. Waking up feeling low, with no energy – I had lost myself again, my self-esteem, my self-confidence, and I had let my body go, also being right back at the start of my loss, it felt so similar. The key was making solid decisions and just putting one foot in front of the other. I thought one thing, though... *I will be back with a vengeance, I promise!*

One major matter, though, from 2021 had been experiencing the true colours of very few around me while attempting to move my life on and find happiness. All, are no longer in my life, and again, it's that beautiful train, folks... some get pushed, but don't be afraid to do it. Choose who you have in your world; some drag you down without you even noticing, and some have a motive, some think they have a right to judge – remove the naysayers in your life immediately.

Starting 2022 with great positivity!

February 2022 – My sanity and mind was the priority

"Life is not about status; status means shit in life… it's about you, how humble you are, and what's important: that is you and your health, full stop."

I will never forget this month. I officially stepped back into Swallows Nest: with so many mixed emotions. I cried most days, felt low, guilty, I had let myself down, I had let Hugo down, and, in a way, I had let Jade down. It was so heavy, I felt very depressed. This step backwards was very emotional, after all I had sacrificed, all my decision-making, all that had happened throughout 2021. I felt like the biggest failure on the planet, but really, I should have acknowledged my bravery and strength; well, I didn't at the time. To step back with Hugo, alone, single parenting again, and doing everything on my own. I will say this though, all that I had done and achieved from Hugo's Birth on my own, I didn't have a doubt within myself.

In this depressed state of mind, I had an ounce of light this month… it was a fresh start, where it all started. It's not about running away; it's about creating a new mindset. The gym was set, as it should have been from when I left in 2021 when it had just been finished. New carpets were down, it was like every little thing in the house had changed, and that wasn't a bad thing; a fresh start came to mind.

Hugo also started at the school in the village he was meant to go to. I will share some feelings around this in the book soon. Trust me, it was so hard and heavy. Taking the journey alone, you will only grow more and thrive, and that was my mission. Remember how special 14th February was, and all the things that had happened on this day – you just can't write this shit, trust me. Well, I am. The house project in 2021 had officially sold on 14th February. I looked up to the stars and said one word, "FATE."

My last pit stop of this month was Jade's inquest. This was the unknown, scary thoughts, facing up to what actually happened, or should I say, as close to the truth as possible. My body, both physically and mentally, went back years, right back to shock, trauma and high anxiety. Dealing with 2021 and the start of 2022 with Jade's inquest broke me inside.

Was I ready for a mental breakdown? YES, crash and burn came to mind again. I broke down at the start of the inquest, I broke down a few times, especially when the pathologist was up talking about Jade; there I was right back on 8 July 2018. But again, I still had this calmness about me, and I was never going to let this go. Trauma in my mind struck again, like never before. I was the first to take the stand, in front of so many, with cameras on me, everyone watching. Having to share what happened through my eyes around Jade, which, let me tell you, was the truth and nothing but the truth. Well, I have a few words to say about the narrative… "Mmmm, I best not. Choose calmness and peace, Ric. Your future self will only thank you."

Jade's inquest will go down as one of the strongest processes I had to go through among so much. I broke down, my mind went right back there, it was what I was carrying at the time. I will say this, though, it brought out the absolute warrior in me. I also know this as well: Hugo will learn what happened to Jade at the right time and age from his Daddy, and Jade will always be in our conversations; she will always be by our side. As it stands, Hugo is at least spared the emotional trauma of the events that led to the loss of Jade (the inquest). Instead, I will continue to provide him with all the love and security for both of his parents, turning negative trauma into positive magic, as his sole guardian.

Home is where the Hart is!

March 2022 – My breakdown

"When we are at our lowest, I guarantee it will not last forever; just try to do you as much as you can, or simply hibernate – just do what's best for you, and you only."

The human brain and body can only take so much, and following all my decisions in 2020–2021: low *self-esteem and self-belief* was what I faced in early 2022, my body broke down. It's just part of the journey – stand among it all, feel it, go through it, but most importantly, find a way to grow past it. Jade's inquest was adjourned till early May, I had to hold onto this for another few months, which wasn't what I wanted. But that's life, we are thrown darts at all angles but it's about how we react, how we respond, how we step forward. Looking back now, I began to break down, pretty much from when I returned home to 'Swallows Nest', materialising into March. Inevitable is the only word I can think of, but I dealt with it myself, moving through it the best way I could, just 'doing' me.

Hugo also started school, my new life would have carried on, but so much that had happened had made me step away. A beautiful lesson in life, realising what I don't want. An experience that sometimes, folks, we must go through. It's hard, it's heavy, but you do get through it. I felt so alone coming back and doing so much on my own. But this represented *strength* and

bravery, I knew this for a fact, and I held onto it. Taking him to school every day was hard, feeling alone, high anxiety, a little **paranoid**. Again, I kind of went back in my mind to where I was six to eight months after Jade died, where I even found it so hard just to go to the local shop. One positive this month, and what felt like a full circle, was that I was off to Vegas again for a wedding celebration. I was so excited for my brother and his fiancée, and it was just what I needed at the time. Also, that grief circle was just constantly spinning, but trust me, although similar processes were happening – bringing back old memories and feelings – I knew I was much further on in my mind than the first Vegas trip in April 2019. I was on a journey of recovery, I was on a journey of small steps to growing and healing. All that mattered was my mind, body, and soul, and this was the start of really investing in me.

My therapy – time with just me and my boy.

April 2022 – Smiling again for me deep inside

"In life when we are hit with loss, trauma, adversity, we learn to see and realise who we truly are, and our own strengths and weaknesses stand out even more."

'Vegas baby', what a start to April this was! Mentally I was a little better, but still felt a little lost in my own life; Jade's case still to face, the unknown – it was all very heavy. Vegas took my mind off it. I drank beer all day, every day, put half a stone on and loved it – getting some big wins too! Not many people walk away and say Vegas, I beat you. I did for sure, and I decided to buy myself a TAG watch, a little treat for me – why not! The wedding and company were epic; what a memory and something I will never forget. The nightclub, Nelly, was 'sick' and me and a friend decided to treat everyone to Nelly tickets and drinks all night from our winnings.

Learning to make time for self-care at the Spa

Being kind and generous felt nice, something I have endeavoured to be throughout my life; humble, kind, and considerate. There's something about giving back, being kind, being there for someone, whether that's just a good ear; it gives me lots of satisfaction – helping people when you expect nothing in return. I even used the spa in the hotel, it was epic and what an experience. I also got a tattoo in Vegas, the king of hearts, the K with a crown above it and a jade green love heart. Why not? A strong symbol that still, to this day, I love.

Throughout the course of 2022, I have never felt loneliness like it. In 2018–2019 I was around lots of friends and family, but even being around most of them could still feel very lonely. 2020 crashed and burned due to Covid, and at the back end of 2020 and into 2021, I stepped forward, made decisions for which I'm accountable, but so are others around me for their decisions and actions taken, especially verbally. Being alone in 2022 was a must for me, and I decided to focus on peace, acceptance and preserving my energy, over anger or bitterness. I had every right to be that way on so many levels, but we have choices in life; choose wisely. I will say it again, folks, step away from people in your life who do not respect your boundaries or wishes. After everything I had been through, any naysayers or negativity was out of sight and out of mind.

My inner peace and energy were more important than anything on this planet at this moment in time. It takes strength to do this; my advice is to be strong or find a way to be around folk that lift you up, support you, back you up rather than poking holes when you're not looking. We live and learn so much after loss, and through my wisdom and being smart came great clarity. We learn about ourselves, but we also learn about others too. We are not here to be liked by everyone, and we are not here to like everyone and agree, like a nodding dog. We are here on this planet to be ourselves; be true to us – that beautiful train, people. I know one thing though for sure, I'm a very smart cookie.

My home is just becoming an even more powerful zone within. What a journey.

Some mornings spent tuning in to paradise beaches and manifesting our dreams

May 2022 – Jade's final inquest hearing

At times in our life, we carry too much baggage, overthink, hold onto what we shouldn't, or even be hard on ourselves. Let it go, trust me, you will feel free; most of the time it's not yours to carry. For me, this felt like the weight of the world.

Wow, so much was going on. A massive project had just finished, *Hugo and Daddy's School Adventures*. I knew I had one more book in me, but also knew this was the end, my 5th and final children's bereavement book for Hugo. It was a great focus through hard times during early 2022 and just what I needed; expressing and doing something **beautiful** for when Hugo starts school. The book really is to **empower** Hugo but also provide as much excitement around school as possible, just what he needs. The book was set for the publishers and was ready to launch on 1 September 2022, the exact day Hugo was starting reception at his primary school! The proceeds of this book were set to go to Misterton Primary School, all for Hugo and to help me. It was amazing working with my illustrator Jackie Tee on this final piece of art: finding the books to watching all the pages materialise; from local spots in the village to the village sign to the school and all the specifics and detail. It is a great book for any kid, and what a journey both me and Jackie had been on within the Hugo and Daddy's saga of books, just beautiful and priceless memories.

Jade's second inquest week was set for early May, my anxiety wasn't as bad, but it was a process of listening to lots of medical staff members' accounts of events. I couldn't believe what I was hearing at certain points. I had to go home and take it on the chin, what I was listening to again, I guess I have to carry that with me forever, but I know one thing, I know exactly what happened, and I choose peace and acceptance over bitterness and anger. I can't live my life like this. I will find a way of letting this go as much as possible, and looking back even now, I've let go of so much, and I'm proud of this. Focusing on self-care and looking after my wellbeing. I was also hit with a huge bill based on the inquest, after going through it all and the heaviness of everything at the end of that week.. Staggering really, but it had to be squared, with no real justice in my mind as of yet. Another heavy banking transfer to deal with to date. I was truly appreciative of my representation though, and all the support they gave, me.

Most importantly I was doing everything I could for Jade, ensuring we had representation, challenging whoever at whatever point through the process.

Juggling the house sale, Jade's inquest and creating the final book for Hugo, to give back!

I also took my last visit to the old house to tidy some bits and bobs up and do a little cleaning while Hugo sat on the stairs, playing. I did what I needed to do – one last check around the house, and I locked up, saying goodbye forever.

The electric gates opened. I also took a photo of me, stood there with my arms up. I did it and was proud of the steps I was taking for me and me only. At times in our lives, we need to do what's best for us and be true to ourselves and our feelings; I was smashing it. I drove away, knowing that completion on the sale was soon and another massive weight ready to drop off my shoulders. As I was driving back home, I had full closure, as the house was only down the road from the hospital. It wasn't easy, but it was also where Hugo was born, which is a better and more positive way of looking at it. My mantra for strength: 'I'm Ric Hart, and I'm a warrior.'

June 2022 – Finding a way to flip negativity into positivity

"Find a way to flip anything heavy into something powerful, inspiring, and create that warmth in your heart. If you can do that, then wow!"

Jade's case hit the national media in early June, and while it was fully expected, it was very hard to see. The reality thrown out to the world and the universe, This was heavy. Was there justice for Jade in my eyes? NO, not yet. I knew I could change the direction of all this, flipping such negative trauma to positive magic. I knew there would be further investigations in the future. How would I flip this negative press, this heaviness? My books? My journey? There was no way I wasn't going to shout to the world about these. I guess it will always be a continuous journey, but it depends how far I want to push it.

Do I see myself sharing my story live on stage or through podcasts? Who knows? It's down to how far I want to go with this and where I am in my life. This is a very powerful story that stays with me and Hugo forever but perhaps can inspire others. Remember one of the biggest currencies out there... you know the rest. I knew, though, the right time would come to flip all this negativity around Jade's case, and having the ability to do this felt very powerful.

Lots of media outlets contacted me, they knew about my book author journey, but I wanted to hibernate, hide away that little bit more, and that's what I did.

Peace, inner peace, and my energy were key at that point, but I knew when the time was right to shout about my journey and story. I was still doing what was best for me and I was very proud of that, staying aligned and in tune with my needs. I was doing 'me' and being true to my feelings, but most importantly, I was on this path of so much growth in my mind, not letting bitterness or anger take over my life, given what I had been going through. I was, for sure, the widowed warrior.

I had also signed up for the 10K 'Race for Life' in Doncaster, which was a great event with friends, always running with my Jade t-shirt on. I guess this will always remain another thing that is non-negotiable throughout my running life. It's an amazing place when you know what is non-negotiable as you grow and with such clarity. I think in life we can compromise too much, and we suffer in the long run. So don't do that, folks, trust me, you will slowly erode.

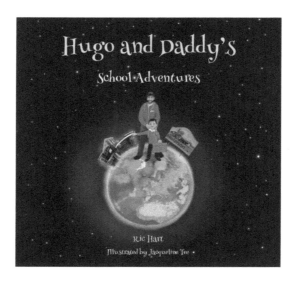

My latest children's book was set to publish on 1st September, with the front cover done, and wow, I must say this was one of my best.

So... the production of my children's books was over. This was my journey and Hugo's, seven books completed as a book author, with all the special elements connected to them. A very unique journey which holds so much emotion, a selfless project to provide a legacy for Jade, for Hugo and self-therapy for me, major steps towards acceptance and healing.

At the end of June, I jetted off for a lads break away to Gran Canaria. The sun was beaming, and it wasn't as busy as I thought, but still great to get away and clear my head a little. The house from 2021 was ready to complete in July, Hugo was finishing for the six weeks holidays soon, *Hugo and Daddy's School Adventures* was set – I loved this final book. What a milestone I had got to, and felt like a million miles away from July 2018 onwards. Wow! We need to focus on how far we have come, not on how far we have to go – a beautiful quote a good friend bought me for my gym wall. Stay in the present, take each day by day. I've come to learn, the past holds you back, the future gives you anxiety, stay in the present and be in the now. What will be will be, but be the best version of you on this planet? – So much that holds us back is unnecessary weight or sometimes the child within us. Finding a way to let it go takes strength, to be happy again, or grow from grief. It is a choice, take that step and don't look back, and of course, it will be a rocky road, but I guarantee years down the line, you will thank yourself deeply.

July 2022 – New territories

Be the best human being you can be for you, grow, love, and influence others positively. This is 100% the strongest currency on this planet alongside time.

This month, I officially let go of all my decision-making from early 2021, and officially let go of what I thought was the right step forward but wasn't. I had to **realign**, make lots of decisions in the background for me and Hugo. I was also making some great decisions in and around our home, with some good ideas for the future. I had my plan and was ready to execute it. Staying on track, alongside training hard, being mindful of me, my heart, and soul. 'Real with Ric', was ringing in my head, as it had in 2021... What was this? My platform to talk out, to share, to help me, to maybe help someone else out there? What platform should I do this on came to mind? I guess I will always be finding my way for the rest of my life, and that's OK. More creativity, more inspiration, more growth.

It was Hugo's 4th birthday, and this one felt lovely; of course, his 3rd birthday had too, for me and Hugo, which is the most important thing. I had left the planning of this one late but got so much done: the cake, the cupcakes, the setting up of Hugo's toy and sweet shop, and Hugo was so excited. We held it at a local farm, which gave Hugo and his friends access to the farm and play area and animal petting. It was a sunny day, and so lovely to see his face so happy. That was a strong moment for me to reflect on how far I had come, all I had achieved in 2022: walking away to be true to myself, realigning our home, creating Hugo's final book for him and making lots of business decisions in the background.

I had also been keeping on top of my health since crashing and burning throughout most of 2022. Then I had low energy and couldn't be arsed to do anything alongside Jade's inquest. What I chose to do is kick myself daily, stay on top of my mental health and physical wellbeing, and keep growing inside. Trust me, this was not easy, but you must keep going or not let grief wear you down for the rest of your life or find ways to grow through it. It was the six-week holidays and new territory for me, with new focus. It was going to be a blast.

August 2022 – Acceptance, healing, and being true to myself

"Test your healing, test your strength, test your triggers; your emotions will only tell you how far you have come. I had come a long way, staying true to me. It's key we do this."

Looking back now from day one of my loss and circumstances, I can say this for sure, I smashed pure inner strength, creativity, and bravery. When we don't have a choice and want to test our own abilities and **manifest** what we want and why we want it, we start to take **powerful** steps, steps towards growth deep within our heart and soul. I lived and still do in the present: I don't worry about next week, I don't think about the past anymore, and I don't overthink the future; this can screw your mind up and create scenarios that haven't even happened yet. Why do we do this to ourselves? I was, and very much still am, in the present. Day by day, hour by hour, being the best full-time Daddy I can be for my son Hugo. Ensuring I'm doing as much as I can to keep on top of our lives for us and to keep **developing**, learning, and putting self-care and wellbeing at the forefront of my life. The healthier and happier I am, the better version Hugo is, and it's as simple as that. Happiness is a choice; find ways to step out of your comfort zone. Do things to test you, allow you to grow, and show the world who you are and what you're capable of.

I remember sitting at the table looking at images of Jade in the hospital, and in the funeral directors. It was something I stayed clear of for so long, but I sat there, just before heading on holiday with Hugo to Spain, and looked at all the images. Deep in thought about where I was and how I felt. I smiled inside with this warm feeling within, saying to myself, "You did it, Ric. You made it this far. You are on a massive journey around healing and sharing, and in some shape or form, your trauma and loss."

I took Hugo on holiday to Spain again in late August, which was the best decision I could have made. When we have been away before, it has normally been with family, but I needed to break this cycle and start to take the right steps forward. This was challenging on my own, but it was the only way for me to keep growing.

I also set up our own YouTube channel, 'Hugo and Daddy's Real-Life Adventures', creating videos of all our trips away. Something for Hugo to look back and remember all we did, but also maybe find some inspiration from. Will Hugo create his own children's book one day and follow the steps of his father? This will be up to Hugo and the universe to decide. I had found peace, I was healing, but I know that I will forever carry the Jade grief stone with me, always. Maybe Hugo won't decide to do his own book, and that is fine as long as he's happy and content. The one thing I know for sure is, though, I am his father, his sole guardian, and life coach, and I will always push him to become the best human being possible. For sure, from the start to this present moment in time, I smashed growth through grief.

Anxiety PAINFUL Journey

Navigate Support STRIVING

Normality Belirve Strength Comfort

CRAZY Creativity

Confused

Ideas Heal Self-care

Relaxation ATTITUDE

Memories Learn

Challenging

Vulnerable Consequences Rollercoaster

Vision

Adrenalin xcitement Happy

September 2022 – Ending the production of the children's books, it's been emotional...

"Focus on how far you have come, not how far you have to go. A place I never thought I would get to, seeing Hugo starting school."

Having to glide through the six weeks' holiday with Hugo, with only one week away to Spain, I can say one thing, that was challenging! But we did so much and created some beautiful memories, our first six weeks' holiday together. Now it was time to start school on the 1st September, and guess what? Hugo's latest book, *Hugo and Daddy's School Adventures,* was published on the exact same day, marking a monumental moment for us both. What a feel-good book for any kid, promoting confidence within school. I remember taking him for his first day in reception, and it was a very emotional moment inside. Jade would be very proud of me, who got to a point he never thought he would, a point in the mountain that felt and looked like an impossible obstacle and a million miles away. But I did it, and I did it my way. Making decisions, making mistakes, learning and growing and gaining huge **wisdom** and **clarity** within. I decided to place the net profits from the book with Misterton Primary School. This gave me a warm feeling inside, giving back and supporting the local community within Hugo's school, every little counts.

Shouting far and wide as I always promised Jade!

At this point, my journey and books started to gain more national exposure, and the *Sunday Telegraph* was one of the sources that wrote about my story. Good for getting our series of Hugo and Daddy Adventure books out there to households that might be going through loss. This will always be an ongoing process throughout my life, and I'm proud of what I've done and whatever steps I decide, going forward, pushing my own journey far and wide. I knew there would be further national exposure around my heartfelt story, but also connected to my book author journey which in itself supports so many causes.

As I look back on my books now and all I have shared, I hope it provides a glimmer of light, showing that in the darkest of places, we can always find a way out. We can do our best to dig deep and show inner strength, creativity and bravery, three elements that will help you to grow, in my opinion, 100%. We can all find a way if I can, the guy who can't read books well at all. I'm no poet, I'm no English literature expert, I'm rubbish at description, I can't spell well, but this is me. I'm doing me, stepping outside my comfort zone, testing myself and sharing something beautiful to the world. I do believe we all have a book in us. This was the moment I truly started to believe I can keep growing, I can keep thinking outside the box, I can keep inspiring others. I can be a representative out there to the world as an idea, not an icon, an idea. We can all find our way, we can all step outside our comfort zone, and we can all find ways to grow deep within our heart and soul.

Never ever give up.

My Story in Summary

As I look back now at my journey of grief through all its stages and everything else that came with it, I 100% believe you will never experience anything else like it in your life. Grief holds its own level of uniqueness for us on this planet. Each person's grief journey holds its own individual set of circumstances: the connection we had to the person we have lost, how we lost them, our personality and character, our values, what we are capable of inside, personal circumstances, support networks, friends, our age. It isn't for us to judge or badmouth someone's steps or decisions through grief. We are not the same person; we are reborn in some way and starting off in life again. With a foundation of loss, shock, trauma, depression, and anxiety, we have to find our way from this point. At a point in my grief I started to loose short term memory, but my god, that rebirth moment, and when my mind came back, I had never felt clarity like it.

My advice to anyone out there is just find a way to be in the present, be true to yourself, don't people-please all the time; it will destroy you. I guess this is natural at the start of your deep grief and shock. Some of those strong connections at the start sometimes fade, and that's OK. It's acceptable to lose yourself, but the beauty in this is you will find yourself again, all in time. There is no rush, and how amazing is this because the only way is up. As I always say, people, it's that beautiful train of life; it takes time, but it's key that you're driving it. Choose wisely who you want on your train, be true to you and what's right because I believe as time goes by, your train of life becomes clearer. I will say this again, be true to you, and do what's best for you; the right ones will come through in the end.

I found a way to accept that being the best version I can be and accepting a new normal provided me with so much power within. I could let go of heavy guilt, which allowed me to grow, and anything else in this life is a bonus. Be grateful for the small things in life: waking up daily and just breathing, it allows you to appreciate so much, and I guess grievers get this a lot.

I will also say this, stepping forward and dating is a massive journey in itself and a huge emotional rollercoaster. Well, it was for me. We may step forward when we are not ready physically or mentally, and we may force things because we are only human. We may not be ready and get hurt or hurt someone else, but whatever we do, go with your gut. If we feel it is working, then go where the energy and feeling is, don't force anything. It's also hard not to get wrapped up in lust, but keeping our feet on the ground and building a strong emotional connection with someone takes time. I experienced all this on the back of a lockdown as well, which cranked things up by 100%.

As I write this part now, sat here in January 2023, with a new year ahead for me and Hugo, there is so much on the horizon. I know one thing, stepping forward and dating again: well, I'm embracing it. I'm in a confident place, knowing who I am and what I'm striding towards, people can either be attracted to me, or they can be a little intimidated, or not be attracted to me, and that's cool. She's out there, but I believe it will happen at the right time for me. It's what me and Hugo deserve, an amazing woman by our side. Either way, making decisions and learning as you go is probably the case through grief. I also felt at times I was looking for Jade in people massively, and that's normal, it really is, but I have to say that I no longer do this. I know what I'm looking for, and I know what isn't right in my new life and my new normal, and that's gold in itself. Jade was an incredible human being and will always be with me and Hugo, but I had to let go of looking for her within others. I guess whatever my second chapter looks like, there naturally will be similarities. Once you don't allow your grief to control you and your decisions, I believe you have found yourself in a very powerful place moving forward in your life.

I remember a friend once saying to me a long while back now, "Ric, she's out there." I believe deep inside my soul, she is. Love conquers all, I believe in this, and I will find my second chapter, and I'm not accepting anything less. They will be amazing, beautiful, compassionate, independent, strong, with a deep soul, and just mega fun to be with. This someone will need to accept me, my past, and what I stand for; this is important to me. I will find her.... or she will find me. Even if this doesn't happen in my lifetime, I've still found a way to accept this and be OK with it. I truly believe in manifestation and the universe.

I will inspire people, having already done so my journey of loss. I will annoy people. I will wi̇ with people's demons because of who I am or maybe because of where they are within themselves. There will be naysayers, people will have made assumptions about my circumstances, and there might be gossip, which did happen through the period of 2020–2022. Never take gossip and Chinese whispers as gospel trust me. I more than likely have spent more time alone with my own thoughts in the last four to five years than most men will do in a lifetime. This has allowed me to work things out over time and just keep growing within. Through grief, we have to be at rock bottom, we have to be reborn again, we have to keep finding ways to breathe better, we have to have that breakdown, we have to fall into deep depression. We feel more than most, and that's OK, but what happens through the other side is we wake up. Having listened, watched, and observed, we learn more about others and also ourselves. It's important we go through this because we start to see who respects us and our boundaries when set and also decisions. We start to see more clearly those that didn't get what they wanted, most definitely finding it difficult to place your happiness among their priorities without an agenda or motive. Through grief, we become a little selfish, and that's OK; it's part of the journey, and peace is the end game.

I don't care anymore about justifying the truth on so many matters, being free of that feeling, a need to explain, well this is growth within. I've aimed to be an amazing human being through my grief and will continue to be that person in so many ways. It's amazing as I write this now, all my decision-making, all the major things that used to weigh me down in 2022, it doesn't weigh me down anymore. I am fully accountable for all my decisions, and I've let go of it all totally; it's not my weight to carry anymore. I'm heading for happiness and living the best life possible with my son and whoever we meet along the way. I believe in who I am, and walking tall is the only way. Why wouldn't I? I'm proud for so many reasons: I stayed true to me, stood firm on right and wrong, and did something truly remarkable through my grief, alongside losing myself and taking steps towards growth and creating the best version of me. This is a lifelong journey for sure.

I found inner strength when I needed it the most because I believed I had something deep inside of me. I survived one of the worst things someone can face. I acted on my creativity and every single idea, my self-therapy, my book journey, and taking steps to healing and acceptance. I'm the guy who clawed back from the gutter in the darkest of places. I didn't want to be alive. I had death on my mind for months, Jade's death, death as I looked into Hugo's eyes every minute of the day for months and all the horrific images of Jade lying in the hospital and funeral directors. I ran thousands of kilometres to assess and release all my feelings to the world and at the same time manifest how I was going to come back from this.

Taking the steps to become a book author, a very ballsy and emotional project, but most importantly, doing it for three people. Shouting far and wide about my books and achievements throughout various media sources, locally and nationally. I have featured many times across BBC radio, men's talk shows, and also mental health shows after lockdown. This takes major strength but steps of growth going forward. I also made mistakes, big ones, and decisions I thought were right at the time, but I also learnt a lot about people around me. I have also learnt so much about myself and what was important to me. I'm wrapped around growth, and I choose to keep growing.

At the beginning of this book, I shared the moment I had placed Hugo next to Jade on the hospital bed in ICU. As I write this now, in January 2023, I can look at this image again of Jade having died on the hospital bed, Hugo next to her, crying. This image is open right now as I write this. I haven't broken at all, looking at Jade. I said to myself, "Wow, Ric, you've come a long way." I have self-healed on many levels, and I'm on my journey of healing even more. The Jade grief stone stays with us forever, but I move forward in my life now, making decisions for me and my son. My grief doesn't control me anymore like it used to, being linked to my decision-making and all that comes with this. I take my grief with me in a very special way, but my decision-making is heavily around what's right for Hugo and Daddy. This is a big step forward within me. What I have created as a foundation for Jade and her memory is spectacular and something that stays with me forever. Turning negative trauma into positive magic for both me and Hugo, and this is the way it is staying, with Jade in our thoughts and discussions at times throughout our lives. There is no way Hugo is feeling major weight on the loss of Jade, as hes the only one without the major emotional attachment, but off course it will affect him at stages in his life naturally, my job is to always make him feel safe and happy. I'm very mindful of what is said to Hugo as he keeps growing as a child, again something I observe, and will have to manage also as his Daddy as time passes.

Right now, my gym is built exactly how I want it, the spa garden is set up with a few final touches, the last addition being a sauna. The ice bath is epic. Feel free to follow my ice bath journey as the widowed warrior on Instagram @richardhart786. The house also has had a full refurbishment from top to bottom, and so Swallows Nest has turned into Ricardo's SPA/Health Sanctuary. Earlier in the book, in May 2021, as I was leaving Swallows Nest, was I looking back at the future? Was it meant to be? Was most of 2021 just a process and lesson I needed to take?

I've built some solid discipline and consistency during 2022, something I know will stay with me always. I have an ice bath at least five days a week, and some weeks nearly every day. It's not easy sitting in 2–3 degrees of ice water for around three minutes each time, sometimes longer, but it's about focus, mindset, discipline and breaking barriers in your mind. Of course, cold water comes with major health benefits alongside speeding up my recovery. Once the sauna arrives, and on my mood board for 2023, is five ice baths a week, five gym sessions a week, and four saunas for 15–20 minutes each time! If I do this every week, the rest of my life will take care of itself. What's that saying again…? Health is wealth! With the solar panels on top of the barn, it's all self-sufficient. I couldn't have been prouder to take these steps and make solid decisions for my health and wellbeing. Remember, too, all the running I did through very difficult and dark times at the start of my loss. Training is now part of my life, but also holds huge emphasis on my journey. Perhaps some would steer clear as it's linked back to something very heavy, especially running. But every time I train now, I visualise my future and see exactly what I want and how I'm going to work towards this. Manifesting at its strongest with deep meaning, and I'm proud. Occasionally I cry and am back there for two minutes, then I'm straight back in the present. This drives me even harder to where I want to be, which means I'm also training faster with so much purpose it's unreal.

I have built a physical and mental sanctuary as a home and am very proud of this; peace and tranquillity come to mind. I feel aligned now, certainly in 2023, with who I am, what I want, and what I know I can offer in this world. I'm doing it now, sharing, talking, being positive and hopefully inspiring maybe one person out there. If it helps me and someone else, that's amazing, and I will keep climbing in my life as time goes on to more growth and more inner peace.

Right from the early days after losing Jade, I knew being a full-time Daddy was important and was going to be 'me' for some time. At times, I did want to step back into my old career and could have quite easily taken a different and perhaps easier path. Going to work and being out the house from 9am–5pm brings huge benefits in the long run after loss. You socialise more, plugging back into normality. You push yourself that little bit more, it allows you to be creative, to have a purpose alongside the life you want to build, and you think differently in your role. It is basically a great distraction and focus for anyone who is going back to work after loss.

I was self-employed, and my whole career crashed and burned after Jade died. I could have gone back, but it would have meant I would hardly have seen Hugo, as being who I am and not doing things by halves, I would have worked 10–12-hour days, building an empire for me and Hugo. I now do this a different way on my terms, making solid business and financial decisions for the coming years while being very much in the present day. I didn't want to be a ghost dad, relying on others stepping in, a nanny maybe or a full-time babysitter, friends, family or settling for a partner just because I needed support. Putting extra stress on myself was 100% not going to happen after all I had been through physically and mentally. My life is about finding me again, being with my son and watching him grow, finding peace and putting my health at the top of the list.

I decided to take the harder route, being full-time to Hugo, going through each day in pain, and grinding with one of the biggest mental battles any male out there could face. It was about the most important thing, watching my son grow and blossom. I will say this, there is nothing more important on this planet than being there for your kids as much as you can, and I chose to be Daddy 24/7, and I'm proud. It must be a horrible feeling to know you haven't been there for your kids, or kid, nothing worse. Consistency with you kids, or kid is very important, showing up, being the best version of you, being in the present, and being a kid again, I guess is key. Spending 95% of my time alone:

making decisions, falling, getting back up, learning, getting on top of my mental and physical health, finding new ways to be creative, dealing with major loneliness, surviving out of a very dark place through my inner strength, it's not easy, trust me. Many would struggle; I certainly did.

The responsibility that I look after now is massive, most wouldn't sleep at night trust me, but I stand very tall now, knowing what and who I want in my life, and I will say this again… she's out there… we will find each other because I will not be single forever; I have too much love to give. Time doesn't heal all, love does, I believe this. My last share on this matter is that I know my inner circle now, and that's a journey in itself. We will trust people, we will see true colours in people at times, and it's our choice what we decide and how we respond. My advice is the smaller your inner circle, the better, especially after loss. Growth through grief is for sure the steps I took from being in the darkest of places to where I place myself today, alongside all my decision-making and what I see as important to my life, and who I choose to have in my life, the bell of growth is dinging massively with pride. Again, I'm fully accountable for my decisions, I've forgiven a few deep down, I hold no grudges, am content with my actions and where I am, but unfortunately you never forget.

I hope you enjoyed reading my story month on month, sharing my thoughts and feelings and processes that happened throughout 50 months of my journey from loss.

Jade's case is still very much pending. As I write this now, I have one final tribunal to attend. It will be very difficult for me, but another huge hurdle that I will be getting over. I've come so far with all this, though, and the truth and heaviness versus my peace and energy. Well, I choose peace over anything on this planet, being very much wrapped around transformation in my life.

Throughout my Journey as I look back now, I wished I reached out to more people who had lost like I had early on, but it's not as easy as that, but where was that in terms of my specific circumstances, it wasn't really, although I did connect with a few folk who had lost their partners to maternal death, There was one chap who I reached out too, and vice versa, and wow the collaboration and similarity of circumstances was just unreal from every angle. People Management, financial affairs, walking away from people, and just general scenarios it was a mirror to a T pretty much. Again, wow it was mind blowing but brought me more peace inside and was just priceless to link myself with someone who got it, fully, absolutely priceless. We are still in touch now, and I hope one day we will meet up. I also am glad I joined Way Widowed and Young, this added value within myself to know I'm part of a setup, that is there to support and understand, which brought me reassurance and comfort, alongside giving back in a beautiful way.

What do the next five years look like for Ric Hart...? My next physical challenge for 2023 was setting myself 600 miles to aim for during March in memory of Jade on my peloton bike around the world, but also for

Hugo. And wow, the fundraiser for the Children's Bereavement Centre and awareness found its way to the BBC news. I couldn't have been more proud.

It didn't just find its way to the BBC news, but I also featured on TV a week later. I couldn't believe it. I will share something with you now, when I was running in 2018, I was running on empty, running away from one of the most horrific tragedies a man could face. But deep within my heart, I said to myself, *Ric, you're going to make it all the way to TV to share your journey and make some powerful decisions along the way*. Hopefully, I will inspire so many by shouting far and wide about a tragic story, how I beat deep grief, and how all my visions and beliefs deep within made this happen. I did it and couldn't have been more proud. Could there be more TV appearances? Maybe. Sharing my journey and decisions and fundraising but also sharing with as many people as possible. We can beat deep grief and do our best to wrap as much good feeling around carrying grief with us for the rest of our lives. I smashed it and did it my way.

Remember, this book is not an answer to healing and acceptance; this is my story. I do believe testing your inner strength and finding ways to grow within and elevate your creativity into action helps massively. Stories help, stories inspire. I truly hope deep down I inspired you or gave you a good feeling inside. Either way, this book, for me, is a win-win because if you felt it and understood parts of it, that's brilliant, but if you didn't, well, that's grief. We can't define grief in a clear, constructive concept, can we?

Follow our journey on **Instagram, @hugoandricstravels @richardhart786** and also Jade's Facebook page for the book, JadeHartPupyLove alongside the website **www.jadehartpupylove.co.uk** and **www.hartshero.co.uk** where you can also buy Hugo's superhero sign on kids' and adults' clothing. I also set up our YouTube page, **'Hugo and Daddy's Real-Life Adventures.'**

I leave you with this thought below, which is my motto and quote through my grief.

We can all find our own way, we just need to fall forward, keep looking up, and truly believe the storm will pass and we will find a way to dance in the rain. Small steps, people, small steps.

Ric Hart (BA Hons)

H for Hope
H for Hugo Hart
H for Hartshero

'Do you have a vision, idea, something that you want to do that is just eating you up inside, take that step, whether it's small steps or large steps, it's not about the destination it's all about the journey. if them steps are small even better"

Ric Hart

My Message to Hugo

Well, where do I start, my boy, from feeding you every two hours from birth to looking after you every day 24/7? Clothing you, washing you, changing your nappies while in the darkest of places deep within my soul. But I did it and kept on doing it for you. You are the reason why I wake up every day; never forget that. Through all my struggles and mental battles through losing Mummy, Daddy found ways to cope with his stress, pressure, deep grief and trauma. I decided to run, and keep running, on empty, on adrenaline, falling to the ground many times. In life, we get hit hard, but it's how we respond, and it's what we decide to do that defines us. You, my boy, in life will be hit with loss, you will be hit with adversity, you will be hit with difficult times, but know this, the juice is always worth the squeeze.

We just have to believe deep within our soul that we are meant for greatness, we are meant for amazing things on this planet, and you, my boy, are for sure. Never let anyone tell you it cannot be done. If you have a vision, an idea, a passion, and it's eating you up inside, go for it, and if you ever need some advice, come to your dad always. I will always be here for you, my boy, to guide you, to teach you, to push you, to elevate you, for you to believe that you were brought onto this planet to do wonders. What that looks like depends on what and where you want to go. We will live a busy, happy life, but I want you to know Daddy will always be by your side. I hope one day when I'm long gone, and you have your own family, wife and kids, you read Daddy's books to your kids and grandchildren. The power in this is immense alongside Mummy's memory, too.

I want to be remembered for inner strength, I want to be remembered for creativity, and I want to be remembered for bravery. You will experience these three things at some point in your life, and trust me, it will enable you deep within. I will teach you, son, as you grow older to find these three elements, but alongside all this to be open with your emotions and don't be scared to share and speak your mind. I visualise now when we are older, I may have found someone special alongside you and your family, and we will have built our own family unit; together, my boy, we will always be stronger. Daddy created a powerful legacy with his seven books, from a tragedy no one should ever have to face in their lifetime. Be you, be different, always believe in yourself, never let anyone put you down, feel your self-belief within and you, my boy, will achieve anything.

The one and only,

Your Dad

Love you, Son. Mummy would be proud; Daddy is for sure.

Long and windy roads lead to
beautiful destinations

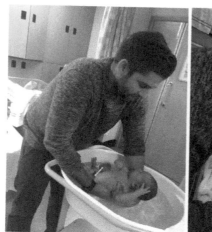
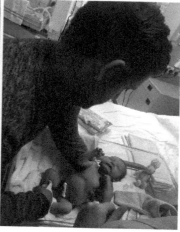

A milestone I never thought I'd get to. Proud!

Jade I never got to say goodbye to you at all after birth, nor did you. Isn't it always the most simplest of day to day things we do that can turn out to be the most heaviest after loss. Never ever take the small things for granted people.. ever.. one day it will be gone. My author journey for sure has lead me all the way up to this point, to now say goodbye Jade. You will always remain in my heart, with strong purpose. We will always be making you proud.